CFRE
Exam

SECRETS

Study Guide
Your Key to Exam Success

Dear Future Exam Success Story:

First of all, **THANK YOU** for purchasing Mometrix study materials!

Second, congratulations! You are one of the few determined test-takers who are committed to doing whatever it takes to excel on your exam. **You have come to the right place.** We developed these study materials with one goal in mind: to deliver you the information you need in a format that's concise and easy to use.

In addition to optimizing your guide for the content of the test, we've outlined our recommended steps for breaking down the preparation process into small, attainable goals so you can make sure you stay on track.

We've also analyzed the entire test-taking process, identifying the most common pitfalls and showing how you can overcome them and be ready for any curveball the test throws you.

Standardized testing is one of the biggest obstacles on your road to success, which only increases the importance of doing well in the high-pressure, high-stakes environment of test day. Your results on this test could have a significant impact on your future, and this guide provides the information and practical advice to help you achieve your full potential on test day.

Your success is our success

We would love to hear from you! If you would like to share the story of your exam success or if you have any questions or comments in regard to our products, please contact us at **800-673-8175** or **support@mometrix.com**.

Thanks again for your business and we wish you continued success!

Sincerely,
The Mometrix Test Preparation Team

Need more help? Check out our flashcards at: http://MometrixFlashcards.com/CFRE

TABLE OF CONTENTS

Introduction

Thank you for purchasing this resource! You have made the choice to prepare yourself for a test that could have a huge impact on your future, and this guide is designed to help you be fully ready for test day. Obviously, it's important to have a solid understanding of the test material, but you also need to be prepared for the unique environment and stressors of the test, so that you can perform to the best of your abilities.

For this purpose, the first section that appears in this guide is the **Secret Keys**. We've devoted countless hours to meticulously researching what works and what doesn't, and we've boiled down our findings to the five most impactful steps you can take to improve your performance on the test. We start at the beginning with study planning and move through the preparation process, all the way to the testing strategies that will help you get the most out of what you know when you're finally sitting in front of the test.

We recommend that you start preparing for your test as far in advance as possible. However, if you've bought this guide as a last-minute study resource and only have a few days before your test, we recommend that you skip over the first two Secret Keys since they address a long-term study plan.

If you struggle with **test anxiety**, we strongly encourage you to check out our recommendations for how you can overcome it. Test anxiety is a formidable foe, but it can be beaten, and we want to make sure you have the tools you need to defeat it.

Secret Key #1 – Plan Big, Study Small

There's a lot riding on your performance. If you want to ace this test, you're going to need to keep your skills sharp and the material fresh in your mind. You need a plan that lets you review everything you need to know while still fitting in your schedule. We'll break this strategy down into three categories.

Information Organization

Start with the information you already have: the official test outline. From this, you can make a complete list of all the concepts you need to cover before the test. Organize these concepts into groups that can be studied together, and create a list of any related vocabulary you need to learn so you can brush up on any difficult terms. You'll want to keep this vocabulary list handy once you actually start studying since you may need to add to it along the way.

Time Management

Once you have your set of study concepts, decide how to spread them out over the time you have left before the test. Break your study plan into small, clear goals so you have a manageable task for each day and know exactly what you're doing. Then just focus on one small step at a time. When you manage your time this way, you don't need to spend hours at a time studying. Studying a small block of content for a short period each day helps you retain information better and avoid stressing over how much you have left to do. You can relax knowing that you have a plan to cover everything in time. In order for this strategy to be effective though, you have to start studying early and stick to your schedule. Avoid the exhaustion and futility that comes from last-minute cramming!

Study Environment

The environment you study in has a big impact on your learning. Studying in a coffee shop, while probably more enjoyable, is not likely to be as fruitful as studying in a quiet room. It's important to keep distractions to a minimum. You're only planning to study for a short block of time, so make the most of it. Don't pause to check your phone or get up to find a snack. It's also important to **avoid multitasking**. Research has consistently shown that multitasking will make your studying dramatically less effective. Your study area should also be comfortable and well-lit so you don't have the distraction of straining your eyes or sitting on an uncomfortable chair.

The time of day you study is also important. You want to be rested and alert. Don't wait until just before bedtime. Study when you'll be most likely to comprehend and remember. Even better, if you know what time of day your test will be, set that time aside for study. That way your brain will be used to working on that subject at that specific time and you'll have a better chance of recalling information.

Finally, it can be helpful to team up with others who are studying for the same test. Your actual studying should be done in as isolated an environment as possible, but the work of organizing the information and setting up the study plan can be divided up. In between study sessions, you can discuss with your teammates the concepts that you're all studying and quiz each other on the details. Just be sure that your teammates are as serious about the test as you are. If you find that your study time is being replaced with social time, you might need to find a new team.

Secret Key #2 – Make Your Studying Count

You're devoting a lot of time and effort to preparing for this test, so you want to be absolutely certain it will pay off. This means doing more than just reading the content and hoping you can remember it on test day. It's important to make every minute of study count. There are two main areas you can focus on to make your studying count:

Retention

It doesn't matter how much time you study if you can't remember the material. You need to make sure you are retaining the concepts. To check your retention of the information you're learning, try recalling it at later times with minimal prompting. Try carrying around flashcards and glance at one or two from time to time or ask a friend who's also studying for the test to quiz you.

To enhance your retention, look for ways to put the information into practice so that you can apply it rather than simply recalling it. If you're using the information in practical ways, it will be much easier to remember. Similarly, it helps to solidify a concept in your mind if you're not only reading it to yourself but also explaining it to someone else. Ask a friend to let you teach them about a concept you're a little shaky on (or speak aloud to an imaginary audience if necessary). As you try to summarize, define, give examples, and answer your friend's questions, you'll understand the concepts better and they will stay with you longer. Finally, step back for a big picture view and ask yourself how each piece of information fits with the whole subject. When you link the different concepts together and see them working together as a whole, it's easier to remember the individual components.

Finally, practice showing your work on any multi-step problems, even if you're just studying. Writing out each step you take to solve a problem will help solidify the process in your mind, and you'll be more likely to remember it during the test.

Modality

Modality simply refers to the means or method by which you study. Choosing a study modality that fits your own individual learning style is crucial. No two people learn best in exactly the same way, so it's important to know your strengths and use them to your advantage.

For example, if you learn best by visualization, focus on visualizing a concept in your mind and draw an image or a diagram. Try color-coding your notes, illustrating them, or creating symbols that will trigger your mind to recall a learned concept. If you learn best by hearing or discussing information, find a study partner who learns the same way or read aloud to yourself. Think about how to put the information in your own words. Imagine that you are giving a lecture on the topic and record yourself so you can listen to it later.

For any learning style, flashcards can be helpful. Organize the information so you can take advantage of spare moments to review. Underline key words or phrases. Use different colors for different categories. Mnemonic devices (such as creating a short list in which every item starts with the same letter) can also help with retention. Find what works best for you and use it to store the information in your mind most effectively and easily.

3

Secret Key #3 – Practice the Right Way

Your success on test day depends not only on how many hours you put into preparing, but also on whether you prepared the right way. It's good to check along the way to see if your studying is paying off. One of the most effective ways to do this is by taking practice tests to evaluate your progress. Practice tests are useful because they show exactly where you need to improve. Every time you take a practice test, pay special attention to these three groups of questions:

- The questions you got wrong
- The questions you had to guess on, even if you guessed right
- The questions you found difficult or slow to work through

This will show you exactly what your weak areas are, and where you need to devote more study time. Ask yourself why each of these questions gave you trouble. Was it because you didn't understand the material? Was it because you didn't remember the vocabulary? Do you need more repetitions on this type of question to build speed and confidence? Dig into those questions and figure out how you can strengthen your weak areas as you go back to review the material.

Additionally, many practice tests have a section explaining the answer choices. It can be tempting to read the explanation and think that you now have a good understanding of the concept. However, an explanation likely only covers part of the question's broader context. Even if the explanation makes sense, **go back and investigate** every concept related to the question until you're positive you have a thorough understanding.

As you go along, keep in mind that the practice test is just that: practice. Memorizing these questions and answers will not be very helpful on the actual test because it is unlikely to have any of the same exact questions. If you only know the right answers to the sample questions, you won't be prepared for the real thing. **Study the concepts** until you understand them fully, and then you'll be able to answer any question that shows up on the test.

It's important to wait on the practice tests until you're ready. If you take a test on your first day of study, you may be overwhelmed by the amount of material covered and how much you need to learn. Work up to it gradually.

On test day, you'll need to be prepared for answering questions, managing your time, and using the test-taking strategies you've learned. It's a lot to balance, like a mental marathon that will have a big impact on your future. Like training for a marathon, you'll need to start slowly and work your way up. When test day arrives, you'll be ready.

Start with the strategies you've read in the first two Secret Keys—plan your course and study in the way that works best for you. If you have time, consider using multiple study resources to get different approaches to the same concepts. It can be helpful to see difficult concepts from more than one angle. Then find a good source for practice tests. Many times, the test website will suggest potential study resources or provide sample tests.

Practice Test Strategy

If you're able to find at least three practice tests, we recommend this strategy:

Untimed and Open-Book Practice

Take the first test with no time constraints and with your notes and study guide handy. Take your time and focus on applying the strategies you've learned.

Timed and Open-Book Practice

Take the second practice test open-book as well, but set a timer and practice pacing yourself to finish in time.

Timed and Closed-Book Practice

Take any other practice tests as if it were test day. Set a timer and put away your study materials. Sit at a table or desk in a quiet room, imagine yourself at the testing center, and answer questions as quickly and accurately as possible.

Keep repeating timed and closed-book tests on a regular basis until you run out of practice tests or it's time for the actual test. Your mind will be ready for the schedule and stress of test day, and you'll be able to focus on recalling the material you've learned.

Secret Key #4 – Pace Yourself

Once you're fully prepared for the material on the test, your biggest challenge on test day will be managing your time. Just knowing that the clock is ticking can make you panic even if you have plenty of time left. Work on pacing yourself so you can build confidence against the time constraints of the exam. Pacing is a difficult skill to master, especially in a high-pressure environment, so **practice is vital**.

Set time expectations for your pace based on how much time is available. For example, if a section has 60 questions and the time limit is 30 minutes, you know you have to average 30 seconds or less per question in order to answer them all. Although 30 seconds is the hard limit, set 25 seconds per question as your goal, so you reserve extra time to spend on harder questions. When you budget extra time for the harder questions, you no longer have any reason to stress when those questions take longer to answer.

Don't let this time expectation distract you from working through the test at a calm, steady pace, but keep it in mind so you don't spend too much time on any one question. Recognize that taking extra time on one question you don't understand may keep you from answering two that you do understand later in the test. If your time limit for a question is up and you're still not sure of the answer, mark it and move on, and come back to it later if the time and the test format allow. If the testing format doesn't allow you to return to earlier questions, just make an educated guess; then put it out of your mind and move on.

On the easier questions, be careful not to rush. It may seem wise to hurry through them so you have more time for the challenging ones, but it's not worth missing one if you know the concept and just didn't take the time to read the question fully. Work efficiently but make sure you understand the question and have looked at all of the answer choices, since more than one may seem right at first.

Even if you're paying attention to the time, you may find yourself a little behind at some point. You should speed up to get back on track, but do so wisely. Don't panic; just take a few seconds less on each question until you're caught up. Don't guess without thinking, but do look through the answer choices and eliminate any you know are wrong. If you can get down to two choices, it is often worthwhile to guess from those. Once you've chosen an answer, move on and don't dwell on any that you skipped or had to hurry through. If a question was taking too long, chances are it was one of the harder ones, so you weren't as likely to get it right anyway.

On the other hand, if you find yourself getting ahead of schedule, it may be beneficial to slow down a little. The more quickly you work, the more likely you are to make a careless mistake that will affect your score. You've budgeted time for each question, so don't be afraid to spend that time. Practice an efficient but careful pace to get the most out of the time you have.

Secret Key #5 – Have a Plan for Guessing

When you're taking the test, you may find yourself stuck on a question. Some of the answer choices seem better than others, but you don't see the one answer choice that is obviously correct. What do you do?

The scenario described above is very common, yet most test takers have not effectively prepared for it. Developing and practicing a plan for guessing may be one of the single most effective uses of your time as you get ready for the exam.

In developing your plan for guessing, there are three questions to address:

- When should you start the guessing process?
- How should you narrow down the choices?
- Which answer should you choose?

When to Start the Guessing Process

Unless your plan for guessing is to select C every time (which, despite its merits, is not what we recommend), you need to leave yourself enough time to apply your answer elimination strategies. Since you have a limited amount of time for each question, that means that if you're going to give yourself the best shot at guessing correctly, you have to decide quickly whether or not you will guess.

Of course, the best-case scenario is that you don't have to guess at all, so first, see if you can answer the question based on your knowledge of the subject and basic reasoning skills. Focus on the key words in the question and try to jog your memory of related topics. Give yourself a chance to bring the knowledge to mind, but once you realize that you don't have (or you can't access) the knowledge you need to answer the question, it's time to start the guessing process.

It's almost always better to start the guessing process too early than too late. It only takes a few seconds to remember something and answer the question from knowledge. Carefully eliminating wrong answer choices takes longer. Plus, going through the process of eliminating answer choices can actually help jog your memory.

Summary: Start the guessing process as soon as you decide that you can't answer the question based on your knowledge.

How to Narrow Down the Choices

The next chapter in this book (**Test-Taking Strategies**) includes a wide range of strategies for how to approach questions and how to look for answer choices to eliminate. You will definitely want to read those carefully, practice them, and figure out which ones work best for you. Here though, we're going to address a mindset rather than a particular strategy.

Your chances of guessing an answer correctly depend on how many options you are choosing from.

How many choices you have	How likely you are to guess correctly
5	20%
4	25%
3	33%
2	50%
1	100%

You can see from this chart just how valuable it is to be able to eliminate incorrect answers and make an educated guess, but there are two things that many test takers do that cause them to miss out on the benefits of guessing:

- Accidentally eliminating the correct answer
- Selecting an answer based on an impression

We'll look at the first one here, and the second one in the next section.

To avoid accidentally eliminating the correct answer, we recommend a thought exercise called **the $5 challenge**. In this challenge, you only eliminate an answer choice from contention if you are willing to bet $5 on it being wrong. Why $5? Five dollars is a small but not insignificant amount of money. It's an amount you could afford to lose but wouldn't want to throw away. And while losing $5 once might not hurt too much, doing it twenty times will set you back $100. In the same way, each small decision you make—eliminating a choice here, guessing on a question there—won't by itself impact your score very much, but when you put them all together, they can make a big difference. By holding each answer choice elimination decision to a higher standard, you can reduce the risk of accidentally eliminating the correct answer.

The $5 challenge can also be applied in a positive sense: If you are willing to bet $5 that an answer choice *is* correct, go ahead and mark it as correct.

Summary: Only eliminate an answer choice if you are willing to bet $5 that it is wrong.

Which Answer to Choose

You're taking the test. You've run into a hard question and decided you'll have to guess. You've eliminated all the answer choices you're willing to bet $5 on. Now you have to pick an answer. Why do we even need to talk about this? Why can't you just pick whichever one you feel like when the time comes?

The answer to these questions is that if you don't come into the test with a plan, you'll rely on your impression to select an answer choice, and if you do that, you risk falling into a trap. The test writers know that everyone who takes their test will be guessing on some of the questions, so they intentionally write wrong answer choices to seem plausible. You still have to pick an answer though, and if the wrong answer choices are designed to look right, how can you ever be sure that you're not falling for their trap? The best solution we've found to this dilemma is to take the decision out of your hands entirely. Here is the process we recommend:

Once you've eliminated any choices that you are confident (willing to bet $5) are wrong, select the first remaining choice as your answer.

Whether you choose to select the first remaining choice, the second, or the last, the important thing is that you use some preselected standard. Using this approach guarantees that you will not be enticed into selecting an answer choice that looks right, because you are not basing your decision on how the answer choices look.

This is not meant to make you question your knowledge. Instead, it is to help you recognize the difference between your knowledge and your impressions. There's a huge difference between thinking an answer is right because of what you know, and thinking an answer is right because it looks or sounds like it should be right.

Summary: To ensure that your selection is appropriately random, make a predetermined selection from among all answer choices you have not eliminated.

9

Test-Taking Strategies

This section contains a list of test-taking strategies that you may find helpful as you work through the test. By taking what you know and applying logical thought, you can maximize your chances of answering any question correctly!

It is very important to realize that every question is different and every person is different: no single strategy will work on every question, and no single strategy will work for every person. That's why we've included all of them here, so you can try them out and determine which ones work best for different types of questions and which ones work best for you.

Question Strategies

Read Carefully

Read the question and answer choices carefully. Don't miss the question because you misread the terms. You have plenty of time to read each question thoroughly and make sure you understand what is being asked. Yet a happy medium must be attained, so don't waste too much time. You must read carefully, but efficiently.

Contextual Clues

Look for contextual clues. If the question includes a word you are not familiar with, look at the immediate context for some indication of what the word might mean. Contextual clues can often give you all the information you need to decipher the meaning of an unfamiliar word. Even if you can't determine the meaning, you may be able to narrow down the possibilities enough to make a solid guess at the answer to the question.

Prefixes

If you're having trouble with a word in the question or answer choices, try dissecting it. Take advantage of every clue that the word might include. Prefixes and suffixes can be a huge help. Usually they allow you to determine a basic meaning. Pre- means before, post- means after, pro - is positive, de- is negative. From prefixes and suffixes, you can get an idea of the general meaning of the word and try to put it into context.

Hedge Words

Watch out for critical hedge words, such as *likely, may, can, sometimes, often, almost, mostly, usually, generally, rarely*, and *sometimes*. Question writers insert these hedge phrases to cover every possibility. Often an answer choice will be wrong simply because it leaves no room for exception. Be on guard for answer choices that have definitive words such as *exactly* and *always*.

Switchback Words

Stay alert for *switchbacks*. These are the words and phrases frequently used to alert you to shifts in thought. The most common switchback words are *but, although*, and *however*. Others include *nevertheless, on the other hand, even though, while, in spite of, despite, regardless of*. Switchback words are important to catch because they can change the direction of the question or an answer choice.

10

Face Value

When in doubt, use common sense. Accept the situation in the problem at face value. Don't read too much into it. These problems will not require you to make wild assumptions. If you have to go beyond creativity and warp time or space in order to have an answer choice fit the question, then you should move on and consider the other answer choices. These are normal problems rooted in reality. The applicable relationship or explanation may not be readily apparent, but it is there for you to figure out. Use your common sense to interpret anything that isn't clear.

Answer Choice Strategies

Answer Selection

The most thorough way to pick an answer choice is to identify and eliminate wrong answers until only one is left, then confirm it is the correct answer. Sometimes an answer choice may immediately seem right, but be careful. The test writers will usually put more than one reasonable answer choice on each question, so take a second to read all of them and make sure that the other choices are not equally obvious. As long as you have time left, it is better to read every answer choice than to pick the first one that looks right without checking the others.

Answer Choice Families

An answer choice family consists of two (in rare cases, three) answer choices that are very similar in construction and cannot all be true at the same time. If you see two answer choices that are direct opposites or parallels, one of them is usually the correct answer. For instance, if one answer choice says that quantity x increases and another either says that quantity x decreases (opposite) or says that quantity y increases (parallel), then those answer choices would fall into the same family. An answer choice that doesn't match the construction of the answer choice family is more likely to be incorrect. Most questions will not have answer choice families, but when they do appear, you should be prepared to recognize them.

Eliminate Answers

Eliminate answer choices as soon as you realize they are wrong, but make sure you consider all possibilities. If you are eliminating answer choices and realize that the last one you are left with is also wrong, don't panic. Start over and consider each choice again. There may be something you missed the first time that you will realize on the second pass.

Avoid Fact Traps

Don't be distracted by an answer choice that is factually true but doesn't answer the question. You are looking for the choice that answers the question. Stay focused on what the question is asking for so you don't accidentally pick an answer that is true but incorrect. Always go back to the question and make sure the answer choice you've selected actually answers the question and is not merely a true statement.

Extreme Statements

In general, you should avoid answers that put forth extreme actions as standard practice or proclaim controversial ideas as established fact. An answer choice that states the "process should be used in certain situations, if..." is much more likely to be correct than one that states the "process should be discontinued completely." The first is a calm rational statement and doesn't even make a

11

definitive, uncompromising stance, using a hedge word *if* to provide wiggle room, whereas the second choice is a radical idea and far more extreme.

Benchmark

As you read through the answer choices and you come across one that seems to answer the question well, mentally select that answer choice. This is not your final answer, but it's the one that will help you evaluate the other answer choices. The one that you selected is your benchmark or standard for judging each of the other answer choices. Every other answer choice must be compared to your benchmark. That choice is correct until proven otherwise by another answer choice beating it. If you find a better answer, then that one becomes your new benchmark. Once you've decided that no other choice answers the question as well as your benchmark, you have your final answer.

Predict the Answer

Before you even start looking at the answer choices, it is often best to try to predict the answer. When you come up with the answer your own, it is easier to avoid distractions and traps because you will know exactly what to look for. The right answer choice is unlikely to be word-for-word what you came up with, but it should be a close match. Even if you are confident that you have the right answer, you should still take the time to read each option before moving on.

General Strategies

Tough Questions

If you are stumped on a problem or it appears too hard or too difficult, don't waste time. Move on! Remember though, if you can quickly check for obviously incorrect answer choices, your chances of guessing correctly are greatly improved. Before you completely give up, at least try to knock out a couple of possible answers. Eliminate what you can and then guess at the remaining answer choices before moving on.

Check Your Work

Since you will probably not know every term listed and the answer to every question, it is important that you get credit for the ones that you do know. Don't miss any questions through careless mistakes. If at all possible, try to take a second to look back over your answer selection and make sure you've selected the correct answer choice and haven't made a costly careless mistake (such as marking an answer choice that you didn't mean to mark). This quick double check should more than pay for itself in caught mistakes for the time it costs.

Pace Yourself

It's easy to be overwhelmed when you're looking at a page full of questions; your mind is confused and full of random thoughts, and the clock is ticking down faster than you would like. Calm down and maintain the pace that you have set for yourself. Especially as you get down to the last few minutes of the test, don't let the small numbers on the clock make you panic. As long as you are on track by monitoring your pace, you are guaranteed to have time for each question.

Don't Rush

It is very easy to make errors when you are in a hurry. Maintaining a fast pace in answering questions is pointless if it makes you miss questions that you would have gotten right otherwise. Test writers like to include distracting information and wrong answers that seem right. Taking a little extra time to avoid careless mistakes can make all the difference in your test score. Find a pace that allows you to be confident in the answers that you select.

Keep Moving

Panicking will not help you pass the test, so do your best to stay calm and keep moving. Taking deep breaths and going through the answer elimination steps you practiced can help to break through a stress barrier and keep your pace.

Final Notes

The combination of a solid foundation of content knowledge and the confidence that comes from practicing your plan for applying that knowledge is the key to maximizing your performance on test day. As your foundation of content knowledge is built up and strengthened, you'll find that the strategies included in this chapter become more and more effective in helping you quickly sift through the distractions and traps of the test to isolate the correct answer.

Now it's time to move on to the test content chapters of this book, but be sure to keep your goal in mind. As you read, think about how you will be able to apply this information on the test. If you've already seen sample questions for the test and you have an idea of the question format and style, try to come up with questions of your own that you can answer based on what you're reading. This will give you valuable practice applying your knowledge in the same ways you can expect to on test day.

Good luck and good studying!

Current and Prospective Donor Research

Influences on Donor and Non-Donor Constituency

Trends and Characteristics of Socio-Economic Status

Wealthy people may be capable of making major gifts, but not everyone can be qualified as willing to use their assets to give extremely generous contributions. An analysis of a list of the wealthiest people in a community and what they give to can provide insight about who the best prospects are for a specific non-profit. For example, it may be popular in this decade for wealthy people in some metropolitan areas to support art museums. A further breakdown of this support may show that wealthy people enjoy being seen as members of an elite group when they contribute in the highest donation amount category. Giving enough money to have a building named for themselves may be judged by many as the ultimate gift by members of the wealthiest socio-economic group. Modest donors may be influenced to increase their giving and non-donors might begin giving as a result.

Trends and Characteristics of Giving Histories

Giving histories can be analyzed to reveal how donor constituencies may have been or may become influenced to make gifts at certain levels. A consistent annual gift made by an individual at the same time every year in the same amount in the same form can indicate a high degree of loyalty to the non-profit. Can that loyalty signal that the donor is ready to be asked to make a larger gift? It depends. What dollar amount does the donor consistently give and what larger gift does the non-profit have in mind? Some development officers may believe that the chances of an increase are small if they ask for too large a jump from one level to another. However, in some cases regular donors can respond positively to a larger solicitation because they are capable and willing but have never been asked. Consistent giving histories also can signal that the donor is a prospect for planned giving, particularly if their annual gifts are modest.

Trends and Characteristics of a Generation

Generational influences on giving are very important to pay attention to. Older alumni of a university may give to their alma mater based on what it used to be. They may not be aware of what kind of university it is today. Older alumni who do understand how an institution has changed may not approve and they may hold onto their gifts in anticipation of it changing. Millennial donors are setting a trend that is asking non-profits to show the tangible accomplishments that result from their gifts. As they analyze the priorities of a non-profit, they may be instrumental in changing its direction. Part of that trend is non-profits inviting millennial donors to participate in hands-on projects so the charity's accomplishments can be keenly felt and appreciated. Over the long term, millennials' gifts may increase as their incomes increase and their involvement drives their donation levels even higher.

Trends and Characteristics of Gender

Conventional wisdom tells development officers that men make charitable gifts to be recognized and admired by their peers, while women make gifts to change and improve something: reducing poverty, accelerating the quality of public education, or changing laws to benefit many people. Non-profits should test their own constituency's conventional wisdom to see if the trends still are valid. Similarly, men may make gifts to support the college teams they played on and the fraternity in which they were active. Men want to stand out. Women, on the other hand, generally do not like to be seen as giving more than other women. For that reason, some women only wish to be recognized at a basic level. They may instruct the non-profit to never recognize large gifts they make. Some women give anonymously for the same reason. It may be difficult for a non-profit to raise

15

continuing funds from a group of men, but more productive to help a women's group sustain their giving for years.

<u>Trends and Characteristics of Culture</u>

Religion can be a significant influence on a constituency because of its belief systems. A social services agency that has been or currently is associated with a religion may draw on donors from church congregations consistently. A college that has been associated with a religion may receive good support from alumni who chose the college because of its affiliation and who were positively influenced by its religious faculty and administrators. Conversely, alumni of a religious college may have formed negative opinions of it because they disagree with the behavior of its leaders and faculty. A religion that takes a strong stance on a public health issue may attract and retain modest and major donors who have strong opinions that agree with the non-profit's position. Religious groups that become involved in influencing politics may develop very strong followings that contribute generously from previous non-donors and donors alike.

Traditional Ways of Acquiring Donors

Traditionally, non-profits have acquired donors by inviting prospects to major events. They have hired well-known speakers to draw crowds to black tie dinners where the non-profit's leaders have spoken effectively about the organization. Guests who are moved by presentations have been known to make their first pledges or outright gifts on the spot or shortly thereafter. Some guests make gifts because it is an unspoken rule that, when a friend invites an individual to a major event, the individual is expected to contribute. National non-profits have run television spots revealing dire needs and demonstrating how the organization is filling those needs. The goal of using television is to drive potential donors to the non-profit's website to make gifts online. The traditional personal face-to-face solicitation has always been proven very effective. Non-profits should consider who at what level does the solicitation. Major donors often are accustomed to being solicited by a president or CEO.

Traditional Ways of Retaining Donors

A rule of thumb in fundraising is that it's much easier to retain a donor than to find a new one. Donors with a consistent history of annual giving have developed habits that non-profits can nurture. Some donors always give at the same time every year, so soliciting them for renewed gifts when it's comfortable for them to give is an easy retention method. Many donors do not like to be called for donations. Coding their file as "do not call" helps make sure campus callers don't irritate them enough to stop them from giving. Other donors do not like receiving direct mail solicitations, so coding them "no mail" heads off what they consider a nuisance that could discourage them from renewing. Many donors appreciate receiving a small gift (premium) every year for renewing. Keeping track of what premiums donors like and dislike generally like helps non-profits offer attractive premiums to retain them in later years. Personal attention to major donors is the best way to retain them. Non-profits compete with others for major donors' gifts, so consistent attention from administrators at high levels is critical.

New Technical Products and Services for Convenient Donations

Websites with online giving pages can offer convenience to some donors who would prefer not to take time to fill out a gift envelope and mail it to the non-profit. For some donors from older generations, online giving may be frustratingly confusing and slow. Non-profits with sophisticated donor databases have the capability of receiving stock gifts online without involving steps that traditionally had been taken by a stockbroker. Some non-profits benefit from crowd funding

mechanisms that enable broad ranges of people to contribute to a website that funds a solution to a specific pressing problem. An example of an old technical process is the telethon. Viewers observe fund drives on television and call in to support the drive with their credit card numbers. It can be a very convenient mechanism for a donor.

Contributing Financial Support to Non-profits

Individuals

Individuals by far contribute the bulk of annual, major, and capital gifts to universities, hospitals, museums, and other major non-profits. Conventional wisdom says that individuals are the largest group to contribute to non-profits because people are motivated by emotion. In many cases this is true. It's certainly a valid proposition in the medical world. Grateful patients and grateful parents of patients have been significant major gift contributors to hospitals and medical research when they have been treated successfully.

Individual donors that seek public recognition for confirmation of their social status often make large gifts to museums, libraries, universities, and symphonies. The same is true for individuals who seek the improvement of their social status and people who want to balance their negative image with a positive one. National charities that produce heavy promotion schedules on television, in direct mail, and online attract many donors that sympathize with victims of unjust or illegal behavior.

Corporations

In comparison to individuals, corporations' share of total giving in the non-profit universe is smaller. In general, corporate giving is not motivated by emotion. Companies budget a specific amount of funding they will donate to charities annually, and staff is required to adhere to their budget. Non-profits generally are aware that corporations will contribute to charities in the areas in which they operate or have large workforces. It generally makes sense for the largest companies to support local charities because they may positively support services for their employees. Corporations may give generously to the United Way to spread their donations across the many non-profits United Way helps. They also may give funding to local universities and hospitals where their employees seek higher education and medical care, both of which help their employees. While companies give charitably to boost their public image, they also are giving to improve their bottom lines.

Foundations

Foundations also can be private, stand-alone organizations that contribute to non-profits with very specific missions that interest them. Families have traditionally established foundations to support their alma maters, children's causes, medical research, and other personal favorites. Large foundations support and encourage global research efforts to cure diseases and to treat life-threatening medical conditions and illnesses. It can be a common myth that private foundations are so wealthy that they can spread their contributions around to help many missions. Most private foundations have guidelines that will inform grant seekers what they will and will not fund. As a source of funding, foundations have never given as much to non-profits as individuals. Corporate giving can decrease when a company's business slows or declines. This applies to matching gifts that companies will make as well as to large outright grant-like gifts that are often paid off over a number of years. Corporate foundations typically operate with guidelines similar to corporations, and they give to non-profits in areas where they operate and where their employees live.

<u>Federal Government</u>

The federal government is a source of very large grants that support non-profit work in areas the federal budget doesn't directly fund. More than 1,000 government grants are generally available in the following categories:

- Agriculture
- Arts
- Business and commerce
- Community development
- Consumer protection
- Disaster prevention and relief
- Education regional development
- Employment, labor, and training
- Energy
- Environmental quality
- Food and nutrition
- Health
- Housing
- Humanities
- Information and statistics
- Law, justice, and legal services
- Natural resources
- Science and technology
- Social services and income security
- Transportation

Federal Project Grant

A project grant is, in general, given to states that award them for scientific or educational research. An example of a project grant would be the Department of Education's Race to the Top. In this project grant, $4 billion in education funding was available. States that applied had to demonstrate they could hire and retain outstanding educators, dramatically improve student achievement, boost state standards, expand charter school curriculum, and improve low-achieving schools. Pell Grants are considered federal project grants. In 2016, approximately 7 million college students applied for and received $26 billion in Pell Grants to help pay for tuition. A third example would be the federal research grant of $4.5 million that was awarded in 1996 to two computer scientists associated with Stanford University for the development of an algorithm for a new search engine that ultimately became Google.

Federal Block Grant

Block grants are often distributed to state governments for extremely large programs that improve human lives through services. A social services block grant funds programs in areas such as childcare, adult daycare, transportation, and substance abuse. It supports mental health and independent living as well as employment training and job placement. Some social services programs prevent and treat child abuse. Unlike some granting bodies that refuse to pay for overhead expenses, block grants will support training and administration. Examples:

- Substance Abuse Treatment - The Department of Health and Human Services (HHS) awards this grant to help prevent and treat substance abuse. States are given money to develop and sustain substance abuse programs through local agencies. The grant targets people who can't afford their own treatments for alcoholism and drug addiction. The size of the state's population influences the amount of funding it receives.
- Community Development - Community development grants are awarded to the Department of Housing and Urban Development (HUD) which administers these grants. They were implemented to solve housing and poverty problems. Each state determines which agencies and programs are eligible.

Categorical Grant

A categorical grant makes up more than 90 percent of the federal grants awarded each year. Categorical grants are awarded for very specific purposes and they are often not meant to fully fund a purpose. Many categorical grants stipulate that the organizations that receive them raise just as much in matching funds.

Federal Infrastructure Construction and Maintenance

A grant may be awarded to a state to build a highway and/or to repair and maintain it. This type of grant might be given for the specific purpose of building or repairing bridges and other critical infrastructure.

Head Start

This grant may be awarded to states to fund their Head Start programs that teach children early skills and get them ready for school; provide nutritious meals; deliver health screenings; and provide medical, mental, and dental services.

Difficulty Obtaining and Stewarding Federal Grants

Federal agencies like to fund work that will become great examples for other non-profits to use as models. While it's possible for an individual to receive a federal government grant, it's not likely. Most federal grants go to organizations. Federal granting agencies are known for their difficult and sometimes burdensome documentation requirements. In fact, some non-profits have been known to abandon their efforts to secure government grants because so much staff time has to be devoted to monitoring and informing agencies of their progress and results. The federal government grant process can be very difficult and is also competitive. Generous funding is available for the skilled non-profits that know how to apply.

Game Nights

Many charities host game nights to raise funds. While gaming nights can be effective, the hosting charities must learn the state laws concerning gaming activities. Auctions are prevalent. The planning committee will ask for donated goods and services to be given for free and, when guests bid on the auction items, the non-profit receives the proceeds. Deductibility is not allowed for successful bidders at auctions or winners of games at charity events. Despite a prevailing opinion among most participants that they have contributed tax-deductible support because it's a charity event, the IRS has ruled that none of it is deductible. In a charity auction, a winning bidder is in fact paying for donated goods or services. At poker nights for charity, for example, people who gamble

anticipate winning a purse. Just like any other charitable gift, the donor must release control of his money without thinking that the non-profit will give them something in return. The IRS calls this a non-quid pro quo charitable contribution.

Identifying Prospects and Planning Solicitation Strategies

A non-profit will search for prospective donors who have a demonstrated interest in its mission, know members of the board of directors and the CEO socially, have been consistently supportive of other similar non-profits, and who may have benefited personally from the non-profit's work. Not all wealthy people are charitable, and not all charitable people have enough wealth to help. However, some wealthy individuals can point a non-profit's leaders to other acquaintances who have the willingness and the capability to give. Modest people who share enthusiasm for the mission with others often can identify prospects that are interested and capable of giving. This identification process can take place at screening and rating events that the non-profit invites donors to attend. Development staff are encouraged to verify the prospect information they glean from screening and rating meetings to ensure accurate data is recorded. Several software companies offer to run programs across a non-profit's donor database to locate helpful information. While this work can be helpful to uncover new prospects, many of them that will be brought to the surface will already be known. Again, it is important to verify the results of a database analysis.

Donor Profiles

Prospect researchers are frequently asked to create profiles on donors and on donor prospects to prepare development directors for solicitation meetings. Development directors will want to know a donor's capability to make a gift. With significant expectations to raise a large amount of funding, a development director wants to spend their time on people who can give the most. Prospect researchers can play an important role in improving the efficiency of the process. To measure and estimate a donor's capabilities, they will identify the donor's occupation and title that will lead them to discovering their salary, stock awards, stock options, and total stock ownership in the company. Other factors include a donor's willingness to give, specifically to the non-profit in question. Information about how much a donor supports other similar charities may be helpful. A development director will also ask for the donor's giving record. How consistent a donor is, how often they increase their gifts, what form their gifts take (cash, credit card, stock, or gift-in-kind), and what the donor has expressed an interest in will help form the strategy. A narrative about who the donor likes in the organization will help suggest who will attend the meeting to make it successful. There is an important factor to include in profiles: is the donor a better planned giving prospect than an outright prospect? Some individuals can leave much more to a non-profit in their wills than they can ever give outright.

Rating Indicators

Indicators in a donor profile may include the donor's address and zip code, title, employer, industry, salary, stock awarded as compensation, major gifts to other charities, estimated value of their home, total confirmed assets, total identified assets, corporate board memberships, foundation board memberships, capacity as a percentage of net worth, and non-profit campaign leadership positions. Information about a donor's willingness to give is just as important as capacity to give. Prospect researchers look at many sources, including Dun and Bradstreet; IRS 990 tax forms; annual reports from universities, hospitals, and museums; county records; real estate; "What It Sold For" columns; corporate annual reports; SEC 10-K reports; foundation websites; non-profit newsletters; university magazines; charity gala photos; and notes from comments made by peers at screening and rating meetings. Profiles also include the names of family members and friends and notes about their non-profit leadership positions, major charitable gifts, and business success. A

development officer may make notes in a profile describing a donor as a planned giving prospect, a major gift suspect, a candidate for an increased leadership role, and recommendations that the non-profit personally visit the donor.

Linkage, Ability, and Interest

If there is a donor prospect that a development officer doesn't know but would like to meet and cultivate, making a cold call to the prospect is unlikely to be successful. The call won't be taken, and a message will not be returned. Instead, the development officer needs a link to the prospect, someone who knows them and can engage them in a conversation. This link could be a board member, someone on the faculty, a member of the prospect's golf foursome, or friends from Rotary. However, development officers should be wary about too much information offered the link. While they know each other, the link may give a development director personal information about the prospect that is wrong, outdated, or misunderstood. Once the connection is made, the development director should glean their own information from the prospect personally. After the connection is made, the development officer should follow up with the link and thank them for their valuable work.

Donor Giving Patterns

A donor's giving pattern may indicate their level of interest in and commitment to the non-profit. A donor who made large gifts in the past but who has not given in five to 10 years may have lost interest. Donors of large gifts may indicate their capacity to increase their giving. A donor who has made many small gifts recently may be indicating they are committed to a non-profit's mission, but their immediate capacity is low. This giving pattern may indicate this prospect is someone who cannot make outright gifts but who could leave a non-profit a bequest. A donor who renews a gift year after year may have done so without being asked. They may make significantly larger gifts if asked. A regular donor who is of an advanced age may have been visited by a staff member who files a report that the donor is alone and may benefit from a source of annual income by establishing a charitable gift annuity or a charitable remainder trust.

Statistical Analysis, Data Mining, and Segmentation

A non-profit's database should be able to generate a great deal of statistical analysis about the donor base. Depending on what kind of database the non-profit has purchased, development staff ought to be able to extract standard reports and write code to create special reports for their purposes. The statistics ought to reveal how donors in different segments are behaving in terms of their giving activity. It may identify trends like diminishing contributions within a socio-economic segment of the donor base. It might show growth within another segment. Development officers can extract information and compare it with statistics about donors in that segment with other similar non-profits or with national figures. This kind of analysis can help development officers discover a segment's potential or identify new donor groups that might fit with the non-profit's mission.

Gathering and Storing Donor Information

Acquiring data about prospects can be done by collecting data about an individual's assets and gifts to other non-profits. Data only tells part of the story. Anecdotal knowledge can paint a very clear picture about things in a donor's background that helps development directors understand them better. This is why a peer group can be important. A volunteer who is willing to part with their knowledge about a donor's family can be invaluable. Timing is everything. For example, it may not be the best time to solicit an individual for a large gift if they are going through a divorce. A wealthy

21

donor may appear to be capable of a large gift, but a volunteer may reveal that they have four children in private schools with expensive tuition. If a member of a peer group is unknown, development officers may interview others to gather personal information. Other information may show up in focus groups when constituents are asked about their opinions about the non-profit. After gathering these opinions, the non-profit may decide to change its approach to marketing, public relations, and fundraising messages to elevate public opinion. The constituency must have a high opinion of the non-profit before a campaign can begin.

Comprehensive Data Management System for Donor Records

Development offices, when looking for a database to help analyze donor information, should focus on several questions. How many individual donors does the non-profit have, and is the database capable of storing all of the donor data with room for growth in the future? What standard reports can the software generate, and which have to be coded for retrieval? How easily can a development director write programs to retrieve more specific information? Does the database have the capability to track moves in the cultivation process? Is it capable of reminding development staff what steps to take next? Can it store the names of a donor's relatives, friends, employers, and business counterparts? What kind of gift ledger does it offer? Can it store many years of personal gifts, fund types, corporate matching gifts, pledges, and pledge payments? Is tech support responsive? Are the firewalls strong enough to prevent a breach of donor data?

Prospective Donor Screening, Rating, and Qualifying

If a non-profit can afford it, screening software can be helpful in identifying good prospects within the donor's database. It also can update the database with current addresses, phone numbers, and email addresses. It can show charitable contributions to other non-profits, real estate values, current business titles, stock ownership, and political contributions. Development directors must remember that, if a donor conceals their wealth within family trusts, no one will be able to find those assets. If a donor database doesn't offer standard programs, screening software can identify donors who are regular and lapsed contributors. Donor databases can include duplicate records and software will help clean those up. It can list donors who are assigned to specific development officers and display a detailed history of contacts with staff. The results of screening software must be verified by development directors who have detailed knowledge of their assigned prospects.

Motivations and Practices of Donors

Individuals

Individual donors are motivated by the mission of the non-profit. They give to support good works, education, conservation, disaster response, animal welfare, religion, and many other worthy endeavors. Individuals make gifts to medical centers after a health crisis. Gifts from grateful parents and grandparents also occur. Individuals will make large gifts for public recognition when they have buildings named for them. Some individuals are social climbers who believe their giving will help them be accepted by wealthy individuals. Friends give to each other's charities as a ritual within their friendship. Many individuals make the bulk of their gifts in the last two months of the year for tax reasons. Conventional wisdom has been that individuals give to charities to reap tax deductions, but research has revealed that most donors don't list tax advantages as their main motivation. They give because they believe in a non-profit's work.

Foundations

Large foundations set policies for how much they will disburse each year, what kinds of non-profits they will support and not support, how many years they will commit to paying off a pledge, and the

22

formats applicants should use. Foundations all have different policies and practices for the grants they award. It's not uncommon for foundations and corporations to receive grant applications through their websites. Other foundations make it clear they don't accept applications from anyone because they support their own favorite charities. Some corporations and foundations only make grants once per year. Others make grants on a rolling basis. The key to foundation support is to read their guidelines and pay close attention to them. Some development directors are convinced that, despite guidelines, they will apply anyway. This is always a mistake, a waste of time, and it can negatively affect morale of a development staff because foundations will discard any letters of inquiry or proposals that don't follow their guidelines. It's the standard practice of some development officers to call foundation program directors and ask them if they might consider a proposal for a grant for a specific purpose. Often the program directors will encourage or discourage them and provide some insight about their policies.

<u>Corporations</u>

Corporations that generously give to non-profits have reasons to be supportive. Arrangements to pay universities for research are common among many companies and science faculties. The research often results in products and services that corporations can sell at a profit. Some private universities depend on revenue from contracts with corporations and actively cultivate relationships. Public universities have been known to seek out research contracts when their funding is cut at the state level. There are virtually no regulations and no oversight for these research relationships and, at the conclusion of a contract, the research findings, products, and services belong to the corporation and not the researchers. It's a common practice for companies to ask researchers to sign non-disclosure agreements that prevent them from revealing their research findings to the public. Sometimes companies build into research contracts some agreements that allow them access to a university campus for recruiting purposes, participate in panel discussions, and attend receptions where they can meet researchers.

Information from Personal Recommendations, Publications, and Online News Stories

Personal recommendations, publications, and online news stories draw a development officer's attention to people who might be potentially generous donors. However, a development professional must dig deeper because of the inherent flaws in these sources. An individual might share that a person is wealthy and capable of making a major gift, but there's no guarantee that the wealthy person is charitable. If the person in question is charitable, they may have no interest in this specific non-profit. A publication may run a story about the success of a wealthy individual. However, the individual may have experienced financial losses since that story ran. Or an individual may have been divorced from a spouse who made them wealthy. Online stories may not be original and may have been taken out of context. That is why development officers must always verify the information they receive about prospects. They must continually update this personal information in case it changes and puts the prospect into a different category.

Annual Giving

Annual giving drives immediate funding for the non-profit. It is an ongoing campaign that runs 12 months a year using direct mail, telemarketing, and personal solicitation. Direct mail is a personalized package containing a letter that asks a donor to renew and consider increasing the gift they make every year. Direct mail should include the donor's name, address, personal salutation, the amount they gave last year, an insert or brochure about the non-profit, and a response device. Response devices can be return envelopes or a website address where the donor can make an online gift. Telemarketing is a program that hires callers or recruits volunteers to call donors, ask them to commit to a gift over the phone, and attempt to get their credit card numbers. If donors balk at providing credit card information over the phone, callers make a note on a pledge card and the development office sends it out the next day. Many employers will match their employees' annual gifts.

Major Gifts

Major gifts mean different things to different non-profits. A major gift at a small non-profit might total $5,000. At a larger organization, it might be $100,000. Major gifts may be raised for unrestricted or restricted purposes, construction, endowed scholarships, endowed professorships, or named funds. Major gifts do not come in as quickly as annual gifts. They take cultivation and relationship building. Generally, a major gift begins with an annual gift, or a series of annual gifts, and it gradually increases as the donor gets to know development staff, becomes involved in the organization's leadership, and takes on significant issues that enable him to see the non-profit's challenges. As they see what the non-profit really needs, donors can become major gift donors if they commit their own resources to solve a problem and build something for the future. Non-profits count on major donors to help attract other major prospects to the non-profit for cultivation, involvement, and solicitation.

Capital Gifts

Capital gifts generally are raised to fund major new construction, boost the endowment, fund new scholarships, and add new programming requiring more staff. Capital gifts are sought during capital campaigns during which donors are presented with many naming opportunities to help motivate them to make significant gift commitments. A non-profit can form a capital campaign to alert donors that the campaign needs people to come forth and help the organization meet its goals. Most non-profits start out with the quiet phase of a capital campaign during which large pledges and gifts are made without announcing them. When a critical mass has been achieved, the non-profit will announce the campaign and report how much money already has been committed to it. This lends credibility to the endeavor and captures the attention of people who may wish to be part of it.

Planned Gifts

Planned gifts come from the estates of individuals who have written instructions in their wills to benefit non-profits. The most common form of planned gift is a bequest. Bequests are normally part of a will and often the largest gifts an institution will receive. Planned gifts also can take the form of charitable lead trusts and charitable remainder unitrusts that are formed to benefit the non-profit and benefit the donor as well. In a charitable lead trust, a donor will put an asset to work for a non-profit for a term of years. Income from the lead trust will flow to the charity and, after the trust ends, the principal will return to the donor. A charitable remainder unitrust provides income to the donor for a set period of years and when it ends the remainder is paid to the charity.

Planned Gifts Used for Income

A charitable gift annuity and a charitable remainder annuity trust are contracts between a donor and a non-profit. The donor buys a charitable gift annuity that is irrevocable in exchange for a guaranteed stream of income for the donor's lifetime from the non-profit. The rate is determined by the donor's age at the time the donor signs the annuity contract and whether the donor is benefitting one person or two. The older a donor is at the time of signing, the more they receive as income. Buying the annuity or creating the charitable remainder annuity trust removes this asset from the donor's estate and helps to reduce estate taxes. A donor also can fund the annuity with appreciated stock and, if it has risen in value, then the donor pays no capital gains taxes on the stock. Older donors like charitable gift annuities because they guarantee fixed payments for life.

24

When the annuity and charitable gift annuity trust donors die, the remaining assets go to the charity.

Relationships Between Annual Giving, Capital, Major Giving, and Planned Giving

Donors do not necessarily make a gift in only one category. The categories are not mutually exclusive. For example, a major donor who endows a scholarship may also contribute to the annual fund in order to support the non-profit's operating fund. A planned giving donor may designate their bequest for capital purposes. Planned giving donors also sometimes contribute annual gifts during their lifetimes. Within the development office, it's imperative that development officers share their assigned donors so they don't become siloed into just one category. In fact, development officers from major gifts and planned giving have been known to meet with a prospect together so donors can hear about more giving options. Annual fund directors should inform planned giving offers about donors who may be good prospects for planned gifts. Annual fund directors should identify major gift prospects as well so major gift officers can plan a visit to discuss their options.

Market Research

Non-profits can go on for years believing that the public has a specific opinion about them. This particular opinion may not be based on anything but internal lore. It is a good idea to survey the individuals who have had some exposure to your non-profit to see how it fares in a focus group.

Useful Methods of Market Research

Focus groups can obtain qualitative information that can reveal opinions that were theretofore wrong or merely unknown. Understanding the results of questioning a focus group can guide a non-profit to creating new images and messages that can boost its support from the public. Sometimes, individuals that think they know what a non-profit does hold opinions formed years or decades ago. As the mission changed, public perception remained the same. Often a non-profit's mission becomes more complicated, serves more people, or gradually gives up work that's no longer in demand as much as it had been. Yet the public thinks of the non-profit in simpler terms with simpler needs. As focus groups prove this is true, the non-profit can expand its communications through its website, fundraising letters, newsletters, magazines, and special events with the goal of raising more money.

In-depth interviews also can be helpful to a non-profit to go beyond comments received from focus group meetings. Non-profits may hire market research experts to select individuals to interview based on many factors. The expenses associated with this kind of research may be beyond the financial capabilities of many non-profits. If a small college decides it needs to do in-depth interviewing, it might present it as a project to a business class that is studying marketing. Faculty can guide the students in methodology so that best practices are used. How the college interprets the results and what it does with the new knowledge gleaned can influence how they retool their marketing or not. For a non-profit to benefit from in-depth interviews, it must be open to hearing new opinions that might challenge management's ingrained wisdom about itself.

Testing marketing materials also can be very helpful when a non-profit is open to experimenting. For example, a development office may write several different scripts for telemarketers to use to discover if new wording produces better results in the number of new and increased pledges. It might deploy new writers to write variations of new direct mail letters and graphic artists to design new brochures and response mechanisms and then to track the results of each package sent to previous donors. A non-profit ought to be very aware of its web presence and testing new messages may be quicker using its website than waiting for results of a direct mail process that can take a

25

long time. The ways in which online giving pages are designed and worded also can be tested to see what versions produce better results.

Laws Protecting Donors' Personal Privacy

A non-profit may have important donor data stored, including debit card numbers, credit card numbers, Social Security numbers, and driver's license numbers. These are generally referred to as personally identifiable information or PII. While there are no federal laws requiring that a donor's privacy must be protected, several state laws require specific information, security measures, data destruction procedures, and security breach notification. For example, the California Online Privacy Protection Act (COPPA) applies not only to websites whose non-profits and their servers are based in California but also to non-profits and servers that reach individual consumers residing in California. The unauthorized use of personal information gleaned from a non-profit in Illinois may be considered a violation of the Illinois Consumer Fraud Act. It also can be considered a violation of the state's Personal Information Protection Act. Because the protection of donor information is not mandated by federal law, it is the responsibility of each non-profit to secure its own donor information.

Using Data Ethically

A donor database is principally used to keep records of donors' charitable gifts to the non-profit. A database also can record many details of a donor's personal life, including salary, total estimated assets, the purchase price of a home, the names of peers and friends, and details of family problems that affect giving. Keeping a donor's information private is so essential that only a few employees should have access to it. A non-profit's adherence to the ubiquitous Donor Bill of Rights makes ethical data handling clear.

Identifying Donor Prospects

The process of locating a donor prospect is called identification and qualification. Development officers spend an inordinate amount of time identifying new donor prospects based on prospect research. Many names may turn up on a prospect list, but many fewer will end up on a donor list because prospects have to be qualified. The process of qualification reviews an individual's wealth, their charitable giving records, their involvement in other non-profits and at what levels, community leadership, their history of gifts to political parties, the number of ex-wives and children, salary, stock holdings, the value of their real estate, corporate board seats, and memberships in private clubs. Only then can one determine if an individual is a potential donor.

Engaging Donor Prospects

Creating a plan for successfully engaging a donor prospect is called moves management. Careful moves will help bring a donor from a medium awareness of the non-profit to the status of major donor. After a donor is identified, development officers have a variety of options to engage them: invitations to hear a speaker on campus, a tour of a major medical facility, an invitation to a symphony concert, or an art gallery opening. The goal of every invitation is to show the donor the best examples of the non-profit's accomplishments.

Cultivating Donors

Cultivation means involvement. Many donors make generous gifts when they participate in hands-on projects designed to help the non-profit. This kind of cultivation helps donors see the needs of the people a non-profit helps. Involvement can also mean giving a donor a seat on the board of

26

directors. Seeing the non-profit from a governance point of view can motivate a donor prospect to form ideas about how they can help in their own minds. Some non-profits send their volunteers out to do public speaking to promote the organization's mission and accomplishments. Universities can put potential donors in charge of class reunions, have them talk about careers with students, do admissions interviews with prospective students, host visitors to the campus, and give them honorary doctorates.

Securing the Gift

Earning and Keeping a Donor's Trust

It's very important for a non-profit to use the right words and graphics to get the attention of the kind of donors it is looking for. Once a donor's attention is captured, it's imperative to demonstrate how responsibly the non-profit is using charitable gifts. A non-profit's integrity and honesty are everything. Donors must feel they can trust the development officer. They will be paying attention to how the non-profit treats them. They must feel that the non-profit is important to them personally before they make a commitment of assets. When they make the gift, donors must feel that the process of giving elevates their own opinions of who they are. In this area, it's imperative that donors be thanked immediately and personally. The non-profit has to keep this feeling going by continuing to pay attention to the donor in ways that are meaningful. Often, the development directors that have been with the non-profit for a long time carry enough institutional memory to provide insight about the right stewardship for individual donors.

Older Donors

When a development officer asks older women to make a planned gift, sometimes they hesitate because they are alone by choice, by being widowed, or through other unforeseen events. Because they only have themselves to depend on, older women often fear they will run out of money if they give any of it away. It's helpful to have a conversation with them about what planned giving is and how they can make gifts that will provide them with income for life. For example, a charitable gift annuity is irrevocable, but the non-profit agrees to pay the donor quarterly income for the rest of their life. Interestingly, when a development officer looks at a calculation of what payment the donor will receive, it can often be disappointing. However, an older donor is often satisfied with the cash flow calculation.

Influence of Emotions Emerging from a Family Crisis on Planned Gifts

When a donor sets up a trust or a gift annuity with assets, these agreements are irrevocable. The donor funds the agreements with assets and they are permanently removed from their estates. Donors have been known to take this step to prevent their children from inheriting their assets. This step may have been motivated by a malfunction in the family that has angered the donor. Because the planned gift agreements are confidential, the children may never know their mother or father put these assets to use. When the donor dies, the assets go to the charity, and that charity has no responsibility to notify family members.

Interference of Donor's Mental Illness on the Solicitation of a Major Gift

A donor diagnosed with a bipolar condition may present moods to a development officer that are very positive and very negative at different times. Similarly, donors with depression may remain depressed for short periods or long periods of time. A development officer who knows about a donor's diagnoses and treatment will be exceedingly careful not to solicit them during a period of extreme positivity when they are cycling or when they are about to go into a depression. Both periods can influence a donor to be extremely generous, perhaps pledging at a level consistent with their capacity or not. Any gifts pledged during an upswing may be cancelled later at a low point in mood. Development officers should be keenly aware of health periods, of time when a donor is rational for solicitation. A family member could be invited to sit in on the conversation to verify the

28

donor's state of mind. Some mental illnesses are impossible to time, including borderline personality disorder, which makes a donor response randomly oppositional.

Influences on Behaviors of Donors

Sociological and Cultural Factors

Donors are lightly, moderately, and heavily influenced by their family background, the culture they come from, the giving of their peers, their religion, their country's attitude toward charitable giving, and many other factors. Some donors give to non-profits because their families always did, and they want to carry on that tradition. In some religions, giving to a church is expected, and church members comply according to their financial abilities. A donor's peers can influence them by calling attention to their own charitable giving. A donor may invite their peers to the dedication of a building named for them, and to awards dinners where a friend is publicly honored for his generosity. Seeing their peers receive adulation may motivate a donor to consider making a principal gift. Within some families, charitable donations are of minimum importance and donors make small gifts. Others may give to a charity without giving it much thought. Discovering a person or a family with dire needs can drive donors to give to Go Fund Me because their friends have brought the needs to their attention. Americans are generous to charities that serve people who have been driven from their homes by natural disasters. They contribute when they see the American Red Cross, the Salvation Army, and other organizations mobilize to help people who have endured floods, hurricanes, tornadoes, and floods.

Religion

Some religions require their members to tithe. Members give a specified percentage of their monthly incomes to their churches. Members who follow this practice are influenced to give by their parents and grandparents who were tithers. Churches launch capital campaigns to expand their Sunday school classrooms, add fellowship rooms, and repair their structures. Church members are actively encouraged to pledge a specific dollar amount to the campaign because the pastor and the ruling council preach what churches call "stewardship." In the development vocabulary, stewardship means something different. Churches that devote a great deal of time and money to mission work ask members to contribute to alleviate suffering and build new schools and clinics. Mission work is a difficult solicitation to refuse. Church leaders may tell their members that making mission gifts is an essential part of their faith. Church members have been known to make gifts to the church because of their affection for their minister.

Household Income, Race, Age, Self-Rank of Social Position, and Marital Status

Household Income: According to a study published by the Wharton School of Business, current household income will influence a donor's charitable giving decisions. However, when an individual has grown up in a wealthy household that was generous charitably in the past, it has no impact on an individual's decisions to give now. Individuals and couples with disposable income may be more likely to be charitable than those who are barely getting by. However, wealthy individuals are not necessarily charitable. Individuals and couples with lower incomes often are more charitable than those with higher ability. In terms of percentage, many low-income families give a higher percentage of their income than those in higher tax brackets. Some of this may be attributable to families who give to their churches; some of them tithe.

Race: Race has virtually nothing to do with charitable giving. Researchers have attempted to analyze giving patterns by race, and many studies have concluded that race makes no impact on non-profit donations. However, the Center on Philanthropy Panel Study (COPPS) researched 7,400 family units and it found that black heads of household and spouses of black heads of household volunteered at a rate that was substantially lower than white household heads or spouses of white heads of households. COPPS also found that when blacks do volunteer, they give substantially more hours to their charities than whites do. While many consultants have written that charitable giving is heavily influenced by volunteering and cultivation, it seems to make no difference in the black community where charitable support of church and other community organizations is very strong and no different from the rate of white support for non-profits.

Age: Individuals and families show tendencies to be more charitable as they grow older. Mortgages have been paid off, retirement funds and Social Security are providing stable income, automobile loans have been paid off, adult children are out of the home, and parents are deceased. With fewer obligations, older people can consider giving more to their churches, their alma maters, community services, and institutions that offer experiences that match their interests. People who are 60 and older are twice as likely to give as younger people. And they are six times more generous. Baby boomers and the World War II generation tend to give magnanimously without asking non-profits for proof of their work. They must be thanked profusely like other groups, but they trust their non-profits to carry out the work they do. Generation X and millennials, however, want to see how their charitable gifts have improved the outcomes of the people who are served. If they don't see enough hard data to satisfy their standards, they will send their gifts elsewhere.

Self-Ranking of Social Position: Many people self-rank their social positions inaccurately. Some underestimate how they rank socially in their communities for many reasons. One reason is that it may not be important to them. Others overestimate how they rank because it is of paramount importance to them. Improving social rankings is one of the strongest reasons individuals make major and principal gifts to high-ranking institutions. This social competition is key to the ability of non-profits to flourish and grow, and it is nurtured in countless ways. If a family seeks social acceptance by the pillars of local society, they may make a significant gift that enables them to put their name on a building, a wing of a building, a college within a university, or to rename an entire university (see Rowan University in New Jersey, which used to be named Glassboro State).

Marital Status: The influence of marital status has much to do with final giving decisions. In the World War II generation, women revealed they had to ask their husbands before making a decision about a charitable gift—even if the gift was only of interest to the woman herself. Baby boomers and millennials make their decisions jointly, but in general they are not seeking each other's permission. One spouse may feel more strongly about supporting a non-profit than the other, and they may pledge for both of them. The spouse making the decision to give will inform their spouse, but since both of them usually are employed, they don't hesitate to give individually. World War II generation women who have their own money from inheritances or from their careers still have to ask permission to give. Baby boomer and millennial women who have their own money don't hesitate to give.

Effective Case Statement

The following are some of the elements of an effective case statement:

- The mission statement-Every non-profit should write a mission statement that makes it clear to everyone what the non-profit does and why.
- The history of the organization-It's important to tell potential donors the story of the non-profit through a narrative of when it was founded, who the founders were, how long has it provided consistent service, and how well it has managed its finances. This demonstrates that the non-profit has been in existence a very long time and that a potential donor can be confident that the non-profit will not close.

- The organization's philosophy on service-Every non-profit has a philosophy of the needs that are significant and its approach to addressing those needs. When a potential donor can identify with the non-profit's philosophy, the chances improve that the donor may make a charitable gift.
- The key services it provides-Services can be very important personally to a potential donor, especially if the services have made a significant impact on them or their loved ones.
- The organization's tangible accomplishments-Potential donors like to see tangible accomplishments, including what needs have been identified, addressed, and fulfilled.
- Testimonials from enthusiasts who have benefited from the organization's work-Potential donors like reading testimonials by people whose lives have been saved, improved, and changed by a non-profit's mission. It demonstrates the non-profit's deep skills and organizational strengths.
- The urgent needs the organization works to fulfill-To persuade potential donors, non-profits must draw their attention to a need that must be addressed urgently. When that urgency is felt by the donor, they will respond with a gift.
- The ways the organization will measure its success-Donors aren't as familiar with the nuances of a non-profit as management is. It's imperative that a non-profit make clear how it measures success and why they're important.
- The organization's future plans-Donors generally don't want to give funding to organizations that may not be in existence in the future. Sharing a non-profit's plans gives donors a sense of its ambitions and implies that it will be operating in the future.

Effective Solicitation Plan

Some individuals believe that development officers spend all of their time asking for money. The opposite is true. Successful solicitations require a great deal of planned activity with the prospect before they can be asked for something. A non-profit would be well advised to create a cultivation plan before it creates a solicitation plan. There are many ways to cultivate a prospect, and they are generally specific to the institution. Development officers might invite a prospect to a symphony concert, a play performance, a tour of a medical facility, or a lecture on anthropology. Development officers should listen to the prospect carefully, find out what is important to them, and offer them tickets to an event that piques their interest. Other cultivation may take the form of informal lunches arranged for the prospect to meet important management of the non-profit. Next comes involvement. When the prospect appears to show an interest in the non-profit, a development officer may ask them to join a committee or a board to show them how the leadership functions. Getting to see the non-profit as an involved volunteer enables the prospect to see the needs up close. As involvement is peaking, the development officer sets an appointment to solicit the prospect. It's very important for the development officer to tell the prospect why they are meeting. This gives the prospect time to think about how much they will give. After the gift is made, the development officer quickly writes a very personal letter to thank the donor. He may ask others to call the donor to thank them. Finally, the development officer must stay in contact with the donor so the model may begin again.

Gift of Appreciated Securities

The law allows a donor to give shares of common stock directly to a non-profit without selling the shares first. If a donor has experienced capital gains in a certain stock, selling the shares would trigger a tax event. The donor avoids paying tax on capital gains when they transfer the shares to a charity. The charity may hold onto the stock in its endowment, or it may sell the stock without incurring a tax event. When a donor gives stock shares, the charity looks for the highest price and

31

the lowest price the stock sold for on the day the stock is transferred. It takes the median price and assigns this value to the gift. This regulation applies to common stock. Closely held shares of private corporations are different investments and are treated differently. If a gift of closely held stock totals $5,000 or more, the stock will be subject to an intense appraisal procedure.

Handling Gifts of Cash

Cash donations should be mailed or hand carried to the accounting department. The accounts receivable accountant will count the amount twice. If it is $100 or more, they will ask another staff member to count it as well. They can document the denominations on an Excel document which contains an Excel formula to total the sum as another means of verifying the amount. If there is enough of each denomination to bundle it, they bundle it in increments, the most common being $20 bills in bundles of 25 each ($500). They print two copies of a cash receipt form, one of which goes with the cash and one of which they keep in a paper file. They take the form and the cash to the staffer who makes deposits and counts it again. If all totals agree, the staffer will deposit it at the bank into the non-profit's account. Cash can be recorded in the general ledger as funds awaiting designation, or FAD, if desired.

Handling Gifts of Property

Non-profits are occasionally approached with offers of gifts of property. Sometimes the description of the property sounds very attractive and, if sold, could bring in some much-needed cash to the non-profit. However, donors have many motives for seeking a charity to take property, especially if it is problematic. For that reason, the non-profit must not accept it without doing due diligence. An inspector should be hired to examine the property. Are there back taxes owed? Is there an environmental hazard on the property? Is there a road to the property? Does it have water and utilities? Is the land buildable? Are there liens against the property? Any and all of these problems might motivate an individual to dispose of the property. If he cannot sell it, a solution might be to attempt to donate it. What if the property comes without encumbrances? Not all charities are capable of disposing of gifts of property and most of the time they don't wish to hold onto it.

Appraising and Accepting Works of Art as Gifts

Donors sometimes offer non-profits works of art that they suggest are valuable. Should the non-profit accept the art? First, the non-profit should review its gift acceptance policies. Next, it would be prudent to review the IRS rules about gifts of fine art. A donor who proposes taking an income tax deduction of $5,000 more must get a qualified art appraiser to suggest the value of the art. The donor must pay for the appraisal. In order for donors to receive IRS approval for their deductions, they must fill out IRS form 8283 and mail it with the appraisal. If a donor wishes to give a work of art that appears to be valued at $5,000 or less, the IRS does not require an appraisal. If the non-profit keeps the art as a teaching tool or as a general asset, the donor may deduct the full dollar amount that the art has gained in value over time. However, if the non-profit sells the art or gives it away, the donor can only deduct the cost basis paid for the art. Artists cannot give away their work to non-profits and receive tax deductions based on their fair market value in the art market per the IRS. They can only deduct the cost of the materials used to create the art, like paint and brushes.

Solicitation Strategies

Minority Groups

Minority groups can make significant contributions to non-profits, but only if they are represented authentically inside the non-profit. They may accept invitations to meet members of non-profits if

32

they recognize the tangible proof of the non-profit's work in their communities. Minority groups are sensitive to tokenism and members want to participate only if their talents seem truly valued by the non-profit. Minority groups are just as generous as members of the white majority. Roughly one third of members of minority groups volunteer and give money to non-profits. Minorities donate a higher percentage of their incomes than upper-income whites. Research indicates that donors who are active in their churches tend to give more. These donors also will give generously to a wide variety of non-profits. However, for a non-profit to be successful at fundraising from minority groups, the non-profit must demonstrate diversity at every level—its board, its staff, and its care receivers.

Women

Women have emerged as the most generous demographic group in the country. A study shows that women in the United States who are baby boomers give more to charity than males in the same demographic. Baby boomer women give 89% more than baby boomer men and 70% more than younger women. Baby boomers comprise over 76 million of the U.S. population and also account for over 90% of the country's net worth. As such, they have significant impacts on non-profits. Women behave differently from men in raising funds. They work collaboratively to raise money to right wrongs and to create positive change in the world. Men typically raise money as a competition with their peers. When the goal is reached, women want to hold a celebration with the group. Men want to name things, in general. Women can be persuaded to return to fundraising and continue to work on projects. Men tend to be finished and move on to something else.

Groups of Men Who Graduated from Same College or University

Development directors have learned over the years that men like to participate in fundraising competitions. For example, in a milestone reunion year, there can be a group of men who want to raise more money for their college than the class that's older or the class that's younger than they are. Sometimes alumni of fraternities at the same college compete to raise the most money in a given year. Men also compete to see who can make the largest gifts to their alma maters. At the top level, men will compete to see who can have buildings named for themselves based on having given the largest capital gifts. Men also are aware of awards given to other men by non-profits, especially when the awards are made at very public and highly publicized ceremonies. Some men believe that chairing non-profit, church, or university committees enhances their status among their peers. As chairs, they are expected to make large gifts to the organization and men who are competitive seek the chairs of the highest-status committees.

Differences in Strategies for Groups of Women and Groups of Men

Women who are alumnae of the same college have said they do not like competing with each other. They don't seek the chair of committees so they can be seen as better than their peers. In fact, the most professionally accomplished and highest-status women prefer to be seen as ordinary members of an alumnae group so they don't alienate their friends. This is why colleges don't ask women in reunion classes to compete with women in others, nor do they suggest that sororities compete with each other. Instead, women tend to set fundraising goals for their groups. These goals might include raising money to help abused women in shelters or funding a scholarship for a student who has financial needs. Development officers sometimes encourage alumnae fundraising groups to focus on needs at the college and not on outside groups. They also encourage alumnae not to fund things the college doesn't need or want, including benches or trees. In contrast with men, alumnae who have met their fundraising goals like to celebrate their success with dinners and honor each other by participating in group photos in the alumnae magazine. Almost no individual women seek any attention for leading the group or for being responsible for its success, again in contrast with men.

Senior Citizens

Older donors are more conservative, less comfortable with risk, less critical of a non-profit's accountability, more attached to what good the organization did in the past, and more respectful of an institution's authority. The development director should offer a variety of conservative planned giving options so the donor doesn't feel their contributions are at risk. They should encourage donors to talk about their experiences in the past with the non-profit because chances are they became involved many years ago. Some donors even began their involvement with the non-profit when they were children. Older donors are more interested in discussing their feelings about the past than listening to the non-profit's activities today. The development director might suggest that the senior citizen make a tribute gift in honor of their favorite professor, doctor, or curator. Leaving a bequest in honor of someone also is something that can motivate older donors. Being sensitive to an elder's comfort zone is critical to a successful solicitation.

Young Donors

Young donors require a different solicitation strategy. Non-profits cannot be aggressive with young donors. They don't have the income to pledge and sustain major gifts, so it's wise to start small. Non-profits that host events for young people to socialize and network will succeed at engaging them and make it attractive for them to return. Young people can be solicited with entry-level gifts by a committee of their peers who want to support causes they care about. When they give as a group, the solicitation is more likely to succeed than an effort at personal face-to-face solicitations which may feel intimidating. Art museums, symphonies, and hospitals have organized young donor group events for decades, and young people in the group are given opportunities for leadership. This is long-term cultivation that could pay off handsomely in the long run when young donors enter their top-earnings years.

Feasibility Study

Before the public phase of a campaign begins, non-profits can create feasibility studies to accomplish several goals. First, the non-profit hires former presidents of universities and other non-profits to make appointments with wealthy individuals in the community. Outwardly, these interviews are set up to ask participants how much money a non-profit could raise within the community. Individuals are flattered to be asked for their opinions and, in the process, they learn a great deal about the non-profit and its purpose. The interviewers listen carefully and let the individuals know they will share their opinions with the non-profit's leaders. In the process, these conversations get the wealthy individuals enthused about the non-profit's work and its upcoming campaign. When the campaign begins in earnest, the interviewees can be invited to lead it and to contribute to it. Thus, a feasibility study serves as a powerful cultivation tool for the non-profit.

Negotiating Gifts

Some donors may not be comfortable making an outright gift. A donor may ask the non-profit to consider accepting a gift agreement that makes it easier for them to pay. Numerous topics can include how many years the non-profit will give the donor to pay their pledge; what kind of assets they can use for payments; and what kind of facility, scholarship, or program can be named for the donor. Donors may want to fulfill their pledge with stock from a private corporation that can be difficult to value. Other donors may wish to donate a gift in kind, and the non-profit has to make a decision to accept it or not. If the non-profit accepts a work of art, will they gain a great deal of money when they sell it? The donor must arrange for an appraisal of the art, pay for it, and share the appraisal with the non-profit. Sometimes a non-profit will be unable to find a donor offering a gift large enough to name a new building. As a result, it may find a donor that can give a lesser amount for the naming opportunity. During a campaign, a donor may be asked to split their gift. One portion would buy a lifetime income vehicle plus an annual gift plus a planned gift that may take quite a few years to come to fruition.

Effects on Social Services Agency's Viability and Services

Many agencies have contracts with states to provide social services to individuals with a variety of needs. However, when the economy slows down, sometimes less revenue comes into a state treasury from businesses. When the state has less money to work with, it commonly suspends contracts. In many cases, social service agencies are the first to be cut. As a result, many agencies initiate layoffs, cut programming, and serve less people as a result. If an agency has foresight, it creates other revenue streams. When those streams haven't been established, it's common for agency management to turn to fundraising to bring in more revenue. However, it's very difficult to raise a large amount of money quickly unless the agency has developed very good relationships with generous donors who understand their mission. Fundraising often doesn't produce immediate results. It's better to lay the groundwork before beginning solicitations.

Motivation for Donors to Give

A donor may be motivated to give because they believe in the non-profit's mission. Their motivation may be to connect socially with other wealthy philanthropists. A donor may give to improve their public image. They may give to lessen their tax burden. Universities, hospitals, and art museums offer naming opportunities—a wing, a lab, or an entire building to name a few examples—to motivate donors to make large gifts. A peer's major gift may inspire their peers to make a major gift, and they may solicit their peers outright for special gifts.

Barriers to Giving

A barrier to giving is a generational belief that a woman must ask her husband for permission to give to a charity. A non-profit may have a mission that a donor opposed in principle. Some donors oppose abortion, campaigns to raise the minimum wage, and immigration rights, among others. Donor prospects have said they will not give to a specific university because it has a very large endowment and it doesn't need the money. Others believe some non-profit CEOs are paid too much. Wealthy people have said they do not give because they do not want to be inundated with solicitations by many charities. A potential donor might feel that, if they give money to a non-profit, it will be less money they can leave to their children. A donor may only own closely held stock in a private company that might be problematic to donate because it may be difficult to determine its value.

Implementing Peer-Relationship Fundraising

Peer relationships can be based on many factors: people who went through high school together, played on the same teams, worked together at the same company, went through undergraduate or graduate school together, are members of the same country club, volunteer together in church leadership, are members of the same professional association, and other backgrounds that bring individuals with a lot in common together. Social and professional peers often influence each other in many ways, one of which is becoming involved in philanthropy. In fact, an individual that speaks enthusiastically about a non-profit can shortcut a peer's interest in it. An endorsement by a peer who is a respected source can create immediate credibility, which helps tremendously in fundraising. A peer's endorsement of a capital campaign can make gift solicitation easier, which is why the successful non-profits fill their boards with highly connected community leaders with wealthy, charitable social networks.

Evaluating Fundraising Programs

Non-profits that have not previously measured their fundraising effectiveness might begin with the simplest measure commonly used by boards: total fundraising net. The non-profit totals the amount it raised during a calendar or fiscal year, subtracts the amount it spent on fundraising, and the total is the fundraising net. The first question the board should ask is: Are we raising enough net dollars to sustain our mission? Normally fundraising is not a non-profit's only source of revenue. Fundraising can be and is used to trim the deficit. However, if the money raised is not enough to keep the organization running, other tools to evaluate fundraising are largely irrelevant. Non-profit boards may also ask what the return on their investment in fundraising is. It is a complex question and an even more complex answer, but a preliminary way to explain it is to calculate the organization's total fundraising expenses, divide it by total fundraising net, and the total will be the cost of fundraising or return on investment.

Measuring ROI

While non-profits don't operate the same way as for-profit organizations, there still is pressure from some donors to prove what kind of return they are getting on their investments of charitable gifts. Non-profits can measure any of their efforts effectively. They can begin by focusing on an established annual event that is very expensive, familiar to donors, and well attended, and that the development team has always questioned the value of. They can calculate all of the costs involved and the total revenue produced by the event. A simple formula would be dividing the revenue by total cost to produce a percentage:

$$\text{Return on Investment} = \frac{\text{Revenue}}{\text{Total Cost}}$$

Non-profits may not have the staff and the time required to calculate the ROI on all of their programs, projects, and campaigns. A third party can be hired to do this analysis so the staff can focus on current fundraising work.

Dependency Quotient and Cost of Fundraising

Assuming a non-profit is raising enough funding to keep the organization running, the board may wish to examine other measurements of fundraising which could raise concerns. One measurement is the dependency quotient. How heavily is the non-profit relying on the continued gifts of its largest donors? Why calculate this quotient? If a small non-profit loses one or more major donors, it could create major financial problems if the organization hasn't built other sources of revenue. It means that the non-profit has not performed enough risk management tasks.

What is used to calculate the dependency quotient? It is the total dollars from the organization's five largest donors divided by the organization's total expenditures. The resulting number is the dependency quotient. The measurement called the cost of fundraising is the total fundraising expenses divided by the total fundraising net. It can be expressed in dollars and percentage.

Average Gift

Non-profits may be asked to report their average gift, formally or informally, to give prospective donors an idea of the size of a typical gift. For example, an average gift of $20 may indicate that the non-profit depends on many small gifts and that it may not have a major gifts program in place. How would a non-profit calculate its average gift? It simply would divide the total dollars received by the number of gifts received. Reporting this number is a basic function. What the board also

could request is the change in the amount of the average gift. How is the change calculated? Take this year's average gift amount and subtract it from last year's amount, divide by this year's amount, and multiply by 100. The board can see the trend over a certain period of years. A non-profit may wish to identify the sources of gifts and which categories produce the most change in the average gift. For example, has the development of online giving increased the average gift size?

Direct Mail

Direct mail is used to prompt current donors to renew their gifts and to acquire new donors. Current donors may have long giving histories. Most of the potential donors on an acquisition list will have never made a gift to the non-profit. The direct mail packages sent to donors are likely to have a good response rate because the donor base already knows the non-profit. For donor renewal direct mail, the response rate averages eight to nine percent. For acquisition mail, the average response rate is one percent. In larger non-profits, the purpose of donor acquisition mail isn't to bring in a large amount of new funding, but to put the new donors into the database so they will be invited to the organization's events. Development officers can meet the new donors and begin to qualify them for potential involvement, which stimulates cultivation. Donor renewal mail is designed with a high degree of personalization with the individual's nickname, perfect personal address, and recent giving history so the donor is aware that the non-profit has taken the time to write directly to them. Donor acquisition mail is mostly not personal.

Gift Agreement

A gift agreement is very important to non-profits that count on the receipt of major and principal gifts during a capital campaign. Verbal agreements may be acceptable at subjacent gift levels. Telemarketing, for example, collects verbal pledges from donors who make annual gifts at the club level. Donors are reminded of their phone pledges and, while most fulfill them, a certain percentage default every year. Instead of attempting to collect the pledges over an indefinite period of time, non-profits write them off. However, they are reluctant to write off large pledges because the campaign depends on them. A non-profit may have had a successful conversation during which a donor has agreed to pledge $1 million. The soliciting team may feel assured that the conversation went so well that the pledge should go unquestioned. A better plan would be to hand the donor a written agreement that they are making the pledge unconditionally to be paid in full within a "time restricted." This written agreement constitutes a contract.

Plan for Paying Pledges

The Financial Accounting Standards Board (FASB) requires that non-profits record unconditional pledges as revenue on the date when the organization receives the pledge (similar to recording bequests on the date when notification is received from an attorney). Donors may elect to pay their pledges in one outright payment, or to pay them off in time using installments. However, because the pledge is recorded as revenue in the year it is received, the non-profit may not record future payments as revenue. This would be double counting. The optimal amount of time a donor usually will be allowed to pay off a pledge is within three years, although some non-profits will agree to five years. Experience has informed senior development officers that pledge periods that run longer than five years may default at some point. This kind of default can be attributed to donor fatigue (a donor tires of making annual payments to a campaign that has ended), a failure of the non-profit to remind the donor of their pledge, or a request by the donor to end their pledge payments early due to financial problems.

37

Using Social Media to Reach Potential Donors and Volunteers

Having a presence on the web can help non-profits increase their visibility. Visitors to their websites can be introduced to their mission, values, leadership, accomplishments, history, facilities, financials, and plans for the future. Every non-profit that can afford to use compelling graphics can draw visitors into their activities which can entice them to become interested in more. The website's compelling images and copy can drive visitors to its online giving form, which should be easy to use, especially for first-time donors. The site also can offer visitors areas to sign up to volunteer to help with events like walk-a-thons, galas, and golf tournaments. Non-profits can be as transparent as possible by attaching annual reports, financials, and 990 tax returns to their web pages and making them easy to open and read. Viewers should be able to contact the non-profit through the website, and staff ought to be able to see viewer's messages quickly and respond.

Communications to Reach Biggest Donors

Non-profits pay special attention to their largest donors using the highest-quality communications pieces. Staff has invitations, brochures, capital campaign packages, annual reports, magazines, honor rolls of donors, donor walls, and photos with biographies on their websites to honor their most important giving groups. When non-profits want to remind their biggest donors of their pledges and annual renewals, they write letters with a significant amount of personalization to acknowledge how well they know them. Letters to these donors will include their names, nicknames, addresses, pledge amounts, payments due, and every letter should include a personal note from the organization's leader. Development officers should load as many personalization details into the donors' files as possible, and they should be reviewed annually to make appropriate changes (death of a spouse or change of address, for example).

Prospect Research

Using Prospect Research to Inform Cultivation and Solicitation Strategies

While prospect research is essential to identifying and qualifying prospects, it also is helpful when development directors are writing cultivation and solicitation strategies. Rather than speculating about what might move a prospect along in these phases, a prospect researcher can help write some specific steps—in partnership with the development staff—that may be effective. Prospect research may reveal, for example, that a prospect may know a member of the non-profit's board well. If that is true, a staff member should be assigned to discover if the two do know each other and how well. Well enough for the board member to invite the prospect to a cultivation event? Research also may reveal that a prospect has extensive wealth and has been willing to contribute to other non-profits. Development officers may decide to invite the prospect to their non-profit's own event that focuses on the donor's interests in art, for example. The extent of an interest the prospect shows in the subject may reveal real or merely perceived interest.

Using Prospect Research Discretely

Development directors must walk a fine line between how much they know about a prospect and how to reveal it for best results. When a development director and a volunteer approach a prospect, it's important to acknowledge the prospect's prominence and some of their accomplishments so the prospect knows the solicitors recognize how important they are. What development directors should never reveal are their calculations of the donor's ability to give, their net worth, the details of their gifts to other institutions, and gossip that refers to anyone the prospect knows. Revealing too much information can make a prospect uncomfortable and divert their attention from the discussion of the non-profit. The development director should allow the prospect to share personal information they are comfortable with. This can help verify what the development office already

knows. Board members and other volunteers who meet with prospects should be advised that prospect information is strictly confidential and that it is never to be shared with anyone.

Direct Marketing

For many years non-profits have communicated directly with donors to remind them to renew their gifts or to ask them to make new pledge commitments. Donors have traditionally received what is called "direct mail" from non-profits. Direct mail is often a package of fact sheets, brochures, a solicitation letter, and a postage-paid return envelope. However, direct mail is a passive form of solicitation. Telemarketing is a more active way of soliciting. Volunteer or paid callers make phone calls to previous donors, asking them to renew and increase their annual gifts. Telemarketers may schedule calls for specific times during the year, or they may call on a rolling basis. Non-profits use email to drive donors to the non-profit's website to make gifts online. Direct response television is a method often used by public television. If a donor sees the program and is motivated to give, they call the public television station and make a pledge over the phone.

Direct Mail

Before a direct mail package can be sent, the development director has much data work to accomplish. They must segment their donors into different categories: last year's donors; donors going back three years, but not last year; donors at any time in the past; and, in the case of universities, non-donors in their alumni base. A basic solicitation is written, and the solicitation wording is changed for each segment. The solicitation amount changes as well. Donors will be asked to renew their last gift, and an appeal for an increased gift is included. Non-donors will be asked for a modest gift. The letter will ask donors to claim matching gifts from their employers. Letters going to donors at the highest levels will be signed personally by the CEO who will add personal notes. Lower-level donor mail and non-donor mail will be sent in bulk. Letters to donors who already have given in the current year must be removed from the mailing.

Telemarketing

In general, data work needs to happen before telemarketing begins. First, the database must be screened for donors who already have given this year. They must be deleted from the telemarketing call lists. For maximum results, callers should begin calling the largest donors first. Most development directors would prefer to see telephone pledges come earlier in the year. Callers work their way down the list, calling the more recent donors first. To build annual revenue, it is imperative to continue to make attempts to reach recent donors because they are the most likely to give. Because most donors will make their annual gifts by December, it is important to reach as many of them as possible before that crucial time. Telemarketing will be followed the next day by mailing out letters to remind the donors of their pledges. Postage-paid envelopes should be included in the reminder package. Some non-profits code the return envelopes for advancement services to track telemarketing results and compare them with other methods.

Direct Dialog

The most effective kind of fundraising is a direct conversation with a donor or a prospective donor. Prospective donors may routinely ignore direct mail and telemarketers, but a call from someone they know is difficult to ignore. Before the call is made, the development director must do extensive research about the person to be solicited. They must have an idea of the donor's title and salary, total investments, family situation, and gifts he has made to other non-profits. It's never a good idea to go into these meetings without understanding as much as possible about the donor. The most effective way to reach a donor is to have a friend of his or a peer make the call and set an

appointment. The friend will go to the appointment with the development director or CEO and discuss their non-profit and what it needs. Donors don't have to give the solicitors an answer on the spot, but follow up is extremely important to close the ask.

Galas and Dinners

It's common for a non-profit to hold special events to raise money as it introduces the community to its mission and accomplishments. Small charities try to create events that rely heavily on volunteers because their staffs are small and busy with their jobs. Volunteers often decide on the theme, the invitation lists, the venue, the budget, and the goal. They frequently run the event as well. Sometimes, the expenses for a special event can be steep. To figure out the success of the event, the expenses are deducted from the amount the event grosses. The total is how much the non-profit keeps. For some small non-profits, fronting the expenses can be difficult, so it behooves them to find a sponsor to underwrite the event. Large universities don't always host galas to raise money. Often, their expenses come close to equaling the gross. Universities use these events to promote good will and public relations with their alumni donors.

Walk-a-Thons, Tournaments, and Auctions

Walk-a-thons have been organized to raise money on the principle that a walker will get a sponsor to pay them to walk for a specific dollar amount per mile. Corporate sponsors of walk-a-thons donate significant support in exchange for having the company name and logo prominently displayed at the event. Golf tournaments charge players to participate and the tournament committee will sell sponsorships. Golf tournament sponsors also will frequently have their company names and logos on display at the event. Frequently, companies will be asked to sponsor a hole on the course, and their signage will appear at the tee. After all of the tournament's costs are deducted, the balance goes to the charity. Frequently, the bulk of funding will come from sponsorships. Auctions are often held during special events like galas, golf tournaments, awards banquets, and trivia nights. Sponsors will donate items to be auctioned, and all proceeds go to the charity.

Formulating Strategies to Apply for Grants

Private Foundations

It may be tempting for development directors to apply to the wealthiest foundations for grants. However, an experienced grant writer will inform the development department and faculty that a better strategy is to do intensive research and find foundations that support their non-profit's work/mission. There are several good sources for this information. The Foundation Center Online is one of the best. Grant writers may search the database by subject, by foundation name, and by state. The Foundation Center Online is the first step. Grant writers should narrow down the foundations that look like a match and go to their websites. There, they may find a number of qualifiers. For example, a foundation may say plainly that it does not accept unsolicited proposals. It may explain that it does not support specific non-profit categories like religious, medical, animal welfare, museum, and a variety of others. A foundation is not required to explain why it excludes some categories of non-profits. Some development officers are often so caught up in their own missions that they may suggest that the grant writer submit letters of inquiry (LOI) to the self-excluding foundations anyway. "If they knew about us they'd support us" is not a good strategy. When foundations state clearly that they don't accept unsolicited proposals, they mean it.

Corporations

In the corporate universe, there are thousands of companies that support non-profits. A development officer's first step is to match up corporations' interests in community support with their non-profit's mission. They should go to the matching companies' websites and learn which division interfaces with non-profits and focus on the employee or employees who are involved. The non-profit may send a simple email to the head of the department with a summary: what the non-profit's mission is, its total annual budget, and what size corporate gift it is seeking. Development officers should not write long emails or attach long documents or videos in this inquiry email. They won't be read or watched. If they're lucky, the corporation will answer the email and plainly decline or encourage. A development officer also can call a corporation's foundation and simply ask if their interests line up.

Government Agency

First, a non-profit should learn if it is eligible for a government grant. Grants.gov is the first place to begin. Government grants require a lot of work, so it's best to find out if your non-profit qualifies. Specific agencies within the federal government make their own grants. They will explain their criteria and the process on their websites. Development officers may register their non-profits through the website before beginning the application process. Grant writers should take the opportunity to thoroughly read the synopsis page and the forecasting page. Agencies will tell grant writers through their EBiz POC (administrator of grants) where their work on their applications may begin and how they will begin and proceed. Development directors and grant writers should read through the agencies' grant-making web pages thoroughly to understand the full process. There are grant writers whose specialty is writing federal grant applications.

Corporate Sponsorships, Partnerships, and Cause-Related Marketing

Total sponsorship of non-profits by North American corporations will reach $23.2 billion in 2017. Competition for corporate sponsorships is stiff. Non-profits have to be smart about the ways in which they contact companies. Non-profits cannot approach corporations the way they approach individual donors or foundations. While management will agree that the mission is important, corporations are more interested in how much sponsorships will boost their bottom lines. They may be fully engaged in cause-related marketing. Corporations partner with large charities to improve their public image and, in the process, lead consumers to a higher awareness of their products and services.

Planned Giving and Bequests

Planned giving means making a decision to defer a donor's gift to the future. There are many reasons to defer a gift. In many cases, a donor can leave a gift to a non-profit in their will that will be much larger than anything they could give during their lifetime. When a donor leaves a gift to a non-profit in their will, it is called a bequest. This comes from the word "bequeath," which means to pass something on or to leave something to someone else. Bequests are written by attorneys for donors and they may be no longer than a paragraph in the donor's will. To be helpful, non-profits readily provide attorneys with specific bequest wording to make absolutely sure the money will be used for the university's priorities and so the bequest cannot be successfully challenged by the donor's family.

Charitable Remainder Trusts

An individual sets up a charitable remainder trust to provide personal income until that individual is deceased. After their death, the assets are given to a non-profit the donor specifies. There is a tax-savings advantage to creating this kind of trust. Once an individual sets up this trust they cannot change it, so it falls into a category called "irrevocable." Planned giving officers will often see the term "remainderman." This simply means the remaining assets. It is important to hire an estate attorney to write a charitable remainder trust. There are charitable remainder unitrusts (CRUT) and charitable remainder annuity trusts (CRAT). The CRAT pays a fixed amount, and the CRUT pays income that can increase or decrease. Not all attorneys have the expertise in estate law or tax law to create a trust that will protect the assets.

Charitable Lead Trusts

A charitable lead trust used to be called a generation-skipping trust. It's the kind of trust that benefits very wealthy individuals. A person sets up a charitable lead trust to put their assets to work for a charity for a specific number of years. When the trust generates income from its investments, the income is paid to the charity every year. At the time the trust ends, the assets go to people who are beneficiaries, commonly grandchildren, but the assets can be paid to anyone. This arrangement saves estate taxes for the beneficiaries. For the most part, a charitable lead trust is only used for very wealthy individuals that pay estate taxes. Currently, individuals have to pay estate taxes if the estate is about $5 million or more.

Inter Vivos Trusts, Testamentary Trusts, and Grantor and Non-Grantor Trusts

In simple terms, inter vivos means an action an individual does while they are alive. Testamentary means something that is done after the individual is deceased, according to their wishes. A grantor trust means that an individual who sets up the trust keeps control of the financial decisions that happen in the trust. The monetary moves they make benefit the person who created the trust. A non-grantor trust is defined as one in which the person who set it up has no control of it. The trustee or trustees make all the financial decisions that happen. In terms of paying taxes, the trustee pays the tax on a non-grantor trust. In a grantor trust, the individual pays the taxes. A development officer's awareness of what kind of trust is set up helps them with conversations with the donor about future plans that can benefit the donor and another entity like a charity.

Major Gift

A major gift means different things to charities, depending on their expectations and needs. A small non-profit may consider $5,000 to be major gift. A museum or university might consider $100,000 to be a major gift. The characterization "major gift" means the difference between an annual gift and one that is larger than most donors give. To determine how a charity defines a major gift, the charity may decide that a major gift is the dollar amount that five percent of its donors is capable of and willing to give. Major gifts are raised by staff known as major gift officers. They're also raised by volunteers who sit on campaign committees. A principal gift is defined as a gift of $1 million or more. Principal gifts are usually raised by principal gift officers. Donors at this level commonly give appreciated assets rather than cash. Universities can name endowed chairs, buildings, or endowed scholarships as a tribute to a principal gift donor. Other special attention also is paid to principal donors. They may be invited to join the board of trustees or awarded an honorary degree as cultivation for their next principal gift.

Memorial and Tribute Gifts

Donors sometimes choose to honor a member of their family or a friend with memorial and tribute gifts. Memorial gifts are often encouraged in obituaries by the deceased's family in lieu of flowers. Sometimes memorial gifts follow the decedent's preference. They might be sent to a hospice that provided care at the end of life, or to the decedent's alma mater. Non-profits that receive memorial

42

gifts must thank the donors immediately because many of them are first-time donors. The non-profit keeps track of the list of memorial donors and it shares them with the decedent's family without reporting the dollar amounts given. For the most part, memorial donors have no interest in the non-profit. Non-profits should not solicit individuals that make memorial gifts because they are most often one-time gifts. Tribute gifts are often donated to mark a friend's birthday or another occasion. Similar to memorial gift donors, tribute donors may only make one gift to the non-profit and they should not be solicited for more.

Hiring Attorneys to Help Make Charitable Gifts

When a donor wishes to give stock, property, or equipment that has risen in value, there may be tax benefits that an attorney can explain. Or the donor might have chosen the wrong type of gift, and their attorney can guide them to the kind of donation that provides the best results. An estate attorney can write a trust to enable a donor to take an immediate tax deduction and other deductions in the future. Attorneys can ensure that when a trust pays out, it is done correctly according to the donor's wishes. An attorney can advise a donor to donate stock that has experienced the highest capital gains to a non-profit in order to avoid paying taxes on the gains. Attorneys also can persuade donors to give away real estate or heavy equipment, for example, and to make special arrangements the donor isn't aware of.

Hiring Financial Advisors to Help Make Charitable Gifts

Donors with large investment portfolios often consult their financial advisors for the smartest ways to make large gifts to non-profits. Financial advisors will take into account donors' holdings of stocks that may be the best to donate. Some stock may have low cost basis and their value has increased so well that the donor would pay significant capital gains taxes if they sell it. Donating it could help a donor avoid paying those taxes and receive a tax deduction. A donor might be advised to pledge a major gift with payments to come from future income. This donor may not need a large tax deduction the year the pledge is made, so paying the gift in installments will provide a charitable deduction every year a payment is received. The IRS does not permit taxpayers to take deductions based on what they will pay, only for gifts they have paid. Financial advisors and attorneys together can make recommendations on tax strategies for major gifts.

Capital Campaign

A capital campaign is commonly created to raise enough money to make capital improvements to a non-profit's facilities. It usually follows the release of a strategic plan that has outlined the non-profit's goals, which may include serving more people, adding more programming, and hiring more staff to work on its expanded mission. The board of directors will have discussed and approved the strategic plan that includes its approval of a capital campaign to help achieve its goals. Before the capital campaign begins publicly, the non-profit will begin a quiet phase during which major and principal gifts will be pledged or donated to form a solid base of support. When it goes public, the non-profit will promote named giving opportunities to its donor base. A table of facilities will inform donors how much they must give to name a building, a lab, a wing, meeting and conference rooms, lobbies, an emergency room, or a performing arts center.

Endowment Campaign

An endowment is an investment portfolio a non-profit used for income to supplement revenue the organization receives from contracts, tuition, and charitable contributions. Some non-profits use most of their revenue to support operational costs and very little is deposited into their endowments in these cases. Universities and colleges have been known to create a policy that says

43

all bequests and trusts that come to the university will be directed to their endowments to help them grow. Not everyone believes in the necessity of an endowment campaign. One that goes on too long will bore the donor base and is likely to fade away. Endowment campaigns should be rare occurrences and most of the large gifts will come from a small number of people, like a capital campaign. Some experts believe that an endowment campaign should be conducted no sooner than every five to seven years. Non-profits should not attempt them unless they have very strong annual and major gift bases and if they can cover deficits with that revenue.

Membership and Alumni Programs

At colleges and universities, the practice of charging alumni dues used to be prevalent. When they paid their annual dues, alumni said they were active members of the alumni association. The drawback to charging annual dues is the lack of growth of the annual fund. If alumni get into the habit of paying a $35 membership fee every year to renew their dues, they won't give more because they don't have to. Attempting to raise more money from dues-paying alumni can be difficult when alumni aren't used to being solicited. Universities and colleges that scrap their dues programs are better able to raise annual giving levels because solicitors can begin with asks for higher amounts. Conditioning alumni to begin giving at higher thresholds can start with the senior class gift campaign. A reunion gift program can raise alumni sites when they are asked to make increased, special gifts in honor of milestone reunions. Capital campaigns also can raise alumni giving levels.

Lottery Games

During some fundraising events, the event manager can offer smaller fundraising games within the event. One of them is a lottery board raffle. While attendees are playing in a trivia tournament, for example, volunteers may walk around and sell lottery tickets. They may be priced individually and discounted for buying a group of tickets. The charity buys $100 worth of real scratch-off lottery tickets and places them on a board. A drawing is held and whoever holds the winning ticket wins the whole board of scratch-off tickets. The non-profit only spends $100 but the payoff for the winner may be much higher. Some charities have written that they sell more tickets than they do during a 50/50 lottery. Volunteers sell tickets. At the drawing, the holder of the winning ticket takes half of the pot and the non-profit keeps the other half.

Restrictions by State Laws when Offering Gambling Games During Casino Nights

Non-profits use gaming nights, often called "casino nights," to attract participants who like to gamble. State laws, however, can be strict. While some states permit non-profits to use lottery games, bingo, and drawings, other kinds of gambling like poker, blackjack, and roulette have been prohibited by some states. Non-profit legal advisors have warned their clients not to gamble with gaming laws. To be eligible, the non-profit must register and submit an application to their state licensing agency to obtain a license to offer charitable game nights. The state agency will investigate the validity of a non-profit's application, including (a) the organization's charitable mission, (b) the intended facility for the charitable games, (c) the integrity of the organization's members, (d) that the gambling activity complies with the law, (e) guarantee that every person that manages a casino night is a volunteer worker for the charity, and (f) proof that the non-profit is licensed to conduct charitable games.

Workforce and Payroll Giving

The United Way has successfully raised money for decades by asking corporations to encourage their employees to give using payroll deduction. Employees have the option of making a pledge for a certain period of time and then fulfilling it by having payments deducted from each paycheck.

44

Every company sets a goal for how much it will give, and employees are encouraged to give generously to reach the goal. Each employee can receive a receipt for their gift when the company reports their donations on the employee's W-2 form at the end of the year. Each donation is made on an after-tax basis, not a pre-tax basis. Employees have options of directing their donations to charities they care about instead of directing them to an unrestricted fund. Some corporations have begun their own workplace giving programs in response to disasters. The corporations encourage their employees to respond quickly through giving by payroll deduction and some employers will match the employees' donations.

Combined Federal Campaign

The federal government operates a payroll deduction program for contributions similar to the United Way. It encourages federal civilian, postal and military personnel to choose a non-profit to support by payroll deduction. The Combined Federal Campaign is the largest workplace giving program in the United States. It currently supports the work of 1,600 non-profits worldwide. The Combined Federal Campaign sometimes hosts mission fairs where non-profits are invited to set up booths to present their cases. They have been known to give employees some free time to attend the mission fair and review the charities. A website also is available to employees to read about the charities they may support. The Combined Federal Campaigns are accountable to the Office of Personnel Management. The Office of the Inspector General audits the Combined Federal Campaign every year to confirm that all employee donations are accounted for.

Community Fundraising

Community fundraising is operated by volunteers that determine its goals and activities. Typically, volunteers will have ideas including setting out jars for cash donations where the public can see them, holding bake sales and car washes, and scheduling concerts. Typically, community fundraising requires a lot of work for a modest payoff. Volunteers can increase the total by writing personal checks and asking friends to do the same. For the most part, community fundraising serves a public relations purpose. The non-profit's name and logo begin to be noticed in the community. Public awareness of the non-profit's work, in general, takes a long time, but when done consistently, it makes it easier to raise larger gifts because the solicitors don't have to explain their mission. For example, the American Red Cross doesn't have to start at the beginning to describe its mission; everyone knows what it does. On the other hand, a small non-profit with a vague name will not be known as well or at all. In this case, the solicitors must begin their work by telling stories about the organization's accomplishments within the philanthropic community. People who have seen its banners and logos at fairs and fun runs may acknowledge they are aware.

Peer-to-Peer Fundraising

When a non-profit wants to maximize major and principal gifts from wealthy donors for a capital campaign, it will emphasize how very important it is for members of the board of directors and other volunteers to solicit their wealthy peers. Making solicitation assignments is not the first step. Cultivating board members and volunteers to lead the major and principal parts of the campaign begins at the inception of the campaign plan. The board will begin discussing the need for a capital campaign after listening to key faculty and staff make presentations. The faculty will already have met to decide what their needs are and their estimated costs. Staff will also have met to discuss infrastructure needs and estimate their costs as well. The board will work with this information, determine the campaign's priority needs, set a goal for capital fundraising, and commission a feasibility study. The individuals who are selected for interviews during the study should be peers of the board members and wealthy persons who give generously to non-profits in the region. These

45

individuals will be asked by their peers to participate in these interviews that will introduce them to the non-profit and get them started thinking about their capital gifts.

The most important element of principal gift fundraising is peer-to-peer fundraising because of all of the factors it implies: respect, trust, family, friendship, mutual support, shared interests, expectations, and empathy. The factors are all emotional and relational. It's difficult to move a prospect to make a major gift by sharing facts about a case for support. However, if a peer shares stories about a need that is addressed by a non-profit, their peer is likely to respect their empathy and listen closely. A peer who thinks highly of a close friend who is a peer may respect them for their financial commitments to their community. Members of a dynastic family known for their patronage of the arts or having university buildings named for them may be significant peers. Sometimes friends will exchange non-profit support. A shared trauma or tragedy may create close bonds between peers, one of whom is likely to agree to make a gift the other solicits for research. Peers who share the same interests are more likely to support fundraising campaigns created to help those interests. Peer-to-peer fundraising in many cases exceeds solicitations by staff or CEOs of non-profits.

Sometimes there are factors at work that may create roadblocks to peer-to-peer solicitations. A peer who feels certain that their solicitation will succeed may not know that their peer has gone through a financial reversal. The peer may not know that their peer is going through a divorce and is unable to commit personal assets to a major gift. The peer who is solicited may have a previously unknown resentment toward the non-profit. A peer who solicits may not know that their peer has made a very significant pledge to another non-profit and their timing is bad. A non-profit may change its policies that the peer who's being solicited disagrees with. A peer may decline a solicitation to pledge because they feel another non-profit with a similar mission accomplishes more. The non-profit's staff can do enough prospect research to discover many of these hidden roadblocks and delete the prospect's name beforehand so peers are not embarrassed by their personal lack of knowledge.

Third-Party Fundraising

Third-party fundraising occurs when an organization outside the non-profit volunteers to do a fundraising event or program for its favorite charity. A restaurant may volunteer to donate a percentage of its revenue on a specific day, or a company stages a special event to help the non-profit. It can be problematic because (1) the event is out of the non-profit's control, which can threaten the quality of the activity and detracts from its public image; (2) although a third party is handling the event, it requires enormous staff time from the non-profit; (3) most of these events pay very little despite the hype of the promotion; and (4) a regular donor may decide to skip this year's gift because they participated in the event. Why can it be unproductive? (1) The restaurant or business that holds the event may unknowingly promote false impressions about the non-profit after the charity has spent decades explaining their true purpose and results. (2) The non-profit's staff will be asked to do significant data preparation, transport premiums with the organization's logo, and figure out registration and parking logistics after already working full days. This staff work detracts from their assigned tasks that provide bigger payoffs. (3) If, for example, a restaurant donates five percent of a $100 check, the non-profit only receives $5. That is not worth anyone's time for such poor results. (4) A regular donor who pays the $100 check may feel good about participating, but she also may decide she's paid the non-profit enough for the year. Her $200 annual gift has been replaced with $5 from the event.

Electronic Media in Fundraising

Using direct mail and telemarketing to raise money is not enough anymore. Many people pay close attention to the web, particularly the sites they enjoy reading, because the content is frequently changed. People have become used to opening email and receiving text messages, some of which can be relevant and some of which are junk. It's the job of a non-profit to break through the clutter and reach an audience of potential donors and motivate them to give their support and not discard the message. Some non-profits accomplish this by asking their viewers to subscribe to their sites where they send out regular updates. Emails that are not discarded by recipients can alert viewers to special events and drive them to the website to register. Text messages do the same. Non-profits maintain Facebook pages for followers that want to keep current about the organization's activity. Media experts have explained that non-profits do better when they have a media presence because there is so much competition for donors' attention and donations.

Relationship Building

Importance of Cultivation to Successful Solicitation

If a development officer makes a cold call on a prospect and solicits them for a charitable gift, the prospect may give very little. In one conversation, the prospect will only learn a small part of what the non-profit's mission is and what is has accomplished. Chances are the prospect will misunderstand part of what is said. The outcome will be a small gift because the prospect isn't involved or invested in the non-profit. Development officers call this process "transactional" because the call isn't intended to cultivate. However, a development officer who spends a lot of time with a prospect has the opportunity to expose them to many facets of the mission, to the dedicated staff, and sometimes to the people that benefit from the services. They can tour the prospect through the facility to talk with staff and see them in action. The staff can tell moving stories about their clients, and this kind of exposure will lead the prospect to respect the endeavor. If this kind of cultivation is maintained for a period of years, prospects can become major donors and effective solicitors.

Elements of Successful Cultivation Plans

Annual Fund Donor Cultivation Plan

Cultivating annual fund donors focuses on making the case for support with descriptions of rewards that can benefit both the individuals that receive support and the donors themselves. A library could successfully make the case that contributions will help sustain a reading program for children and, in return, the library will send out coffee mugs to donors as a thank you gift. Once a donor's name and gift are entered into the non-profit's database, the donor can be added to mailing lists for newsletters, magazines, invitations to events, and appeal letters. The more a donor knows about the non-profit and the more they are reminded of the non-profit's good works, the greater the likelihood of renewing and increasing their gift becomes.

Major Gift Donor Cultivation Plan

A cultivation plan is best when it is based on the donor's interests and the ability of the non-profit to provide access to those interests. For example, if a donor is interested in music, a development officer may invite them to a classical music concert on campus. As development officers get to know donors better, they can create lists of the things a donor has an interest in. They also can draw up a list of events, performances, lectures, or openings they've taken them to. Major donors can be invited to speak to a college class, impart their knowledge, and talk with students. They could take a hospital tour and meet patients. A development officer could ask them to join a capital campaign committee to get them invested in building new buildings. From their view from the committee they can feel like insiders and they can get a very intensive look at the non-profit's needs. Typically moving a donor from an annual gift up to successfully soliciting a major gift of $1 million or more takes 20 years of cultivation and involvement.

Planned Giving Donor Cultivation Plan

Understanding the non-profit's mission today and how it plans to grow helps a planned giving donor and prospect think about what they can do to help. Often a planned giving prospect will reveal that they cannot make a major gift from their assets, but they're dedicated to the mission and they want to help support it. A planned giving director might introduce estate planning options to them as well as life income gifts. Because they can be complicated, it helps if a planned giving prospect can take time to read through estate planning options and discuss them with their

48

attorney. As cultivation continues, prospects will be invited to experience different facets of the non-profit's work. They may be particularly touched by the people the non-profit cares for at some point, and the staff as well. It's common for prospects to write bequests into their wills at some point during cultivation—and not notify the non-profit. Most donors are private about their estate plans and do not want to reveal them because they don't want a lot of attention. On the other hand, some planned giving donors relish the ways in which non-profits can honor them. The cultivation of a planned giving donor can continue for decades before they make a decision, so conventional wisdom advises staff to keep including prospects in everything.

Goals of Comprehensive Communications Plan

Designing a comprehensive communications plan is more than just following a publication schedule. The non-profit should create goals for its communications work. What are its target audiences? How does an organization communicate best with these audiences? What results is it looking for? Is it a university whose goal is to increase enrollment? Would it be a non-profit that wants to develop more programs to serve more people? Maybe it is a college that wants to build more buildings to expand classroom and lab space. A non-profit should write its criteria for metrics to measure its progress toward its goals. The plan may receive additional funding from the administration to reach them. Additional funding may enable the hiring of additional staff, support the upgrade of its website, and print more substantial collateral materials. It also may include more media exposure and more travel for key administrators involved in the plan.

Deciding Reach and Range of Communications

Deciding the range and reach of communications starts with the board of directors. During the creation or revision of a strategic plan, the board can discuss the possibility of the organization strengthening its efforts to recruit more students, serve heretofore underserved populations, reaching out to countries outside the United States, or join forces with other non-profits to address political issues. The board, however, should include the non-profit's CEO, communications director, and any consultants it values to create the plan according to professional standards and a realistic timeline. After the board gives its approval, the CEO and their team will write the new plan with their goals, staff required, vendors selected, a budget, and metrics to be used for measuring progress and results. When working with other non-profits, the CEO and staff will have to coordinate their work with other non-profits' staff. The best practice is to select a leader who has experience conducting coordinating campaigns.

Basic Donor Acquisition Strategies

It's much more difficult to acquire a new donor than to retain a consistent donor. There is a lot of competition in the community for non-profit support. With universities, megachurches, art museums, medical centers, symphonies, private schools, and other large non-profits campaigning intensely for major gifts in a community, it's difficult for smaller non-profits to get and hold the attention of generous donors. Often, they can offer things to potential donors that others don't. Small non-profits have been known to use board connections to bring in celebrities and famous athletes to host galas, with opportunities for attendees to meet them. Board members and presidents use their season tickets to invite prospective donors to join them at baseball games, symphonies, football games, plays, and musicals. Non-profit leaders also can invite potential donors to accompany them on fishing and hunting trips. Individuals have opportunities to get to know executives of small non-profits. Large universities and medical centers may not offer such personal cultivation.

Acquiring New Planned Giving Donors

It has been a standard practice for a long time to send planned giving newsletters to donors and prospects. The newsletters contain information about planned gift instruments to inform recipients about options for giving. Typically, non-profits contract with planned giving consultants who print the newsletters with pre-printed articles and then they insert the name of the planned giving director, their phone number, email address, and sometimes a short form that the recipients can fill out and mail to the non-profit. Planned giving newsletters work well for some non-profits, less well for others. One view of the newsletter is that it plants a seed in donors' minds. They may be moved to ask their attorneys to write bequests in their wills. They might call several non-profits and ask what interest rate they are paying on charitable gift annuities. All non-profits are supposed to quote the same interest rate for people of the same age, but it can vary. Some non-profits will quote a bit higher to get the annuity contract. Donors even will name a number and ask the non-profit to meet it. Every charity must decide what it can do.

Gratitude as an Important Donor Retention Strategy

There are really no quick and easy ways to retain a donor. It requires consistent work. The first step is to thank the donor immediately by phone and by mail as soon as the gift is received. Donors expect to feel appreciated. If the development officer can express true gratitude, the donor will know someone noticed the gift when it came in and that it's important. Next, donors commonly complain that the only time they hear from the non-profit is when it needs more money. This is why making contact socially with the donor throughout the year in ways that are not transactional really helps staying connected.

When a donor gives to a children's charity, they might appreciate receiving a photo of the child or a picture the child has drawn for them. Taking the picture to the donor and talking about the child can be great reason for contact, and it may be something more personal than other charities do for the same donor. Asking a scholarship recipient or a food pantry recipient to write personal notecards in which they thank the donor and signing them really makes in impact. Donors become personally introduced to the recipients who, up until that point, were only abstract figures in the cover of a brochure or headlining a website page. Although it's done commonly, inviting a donor to an annual dinner with 300 other people or sending out a tote bag are not very effective in retaining excellent donors for the very long term because every non-profit does it.

Less-Than-Personal Approaches to Solicitation of Donors

When a non-profit is approaching non-donors or donors who give at a minimal level, it often sends a direct mail letter asking a donor to make a gift. This is a less-than-personal solicitation. A non-personalized direct mail letter typically has a low response rate and it may not be very effective for soliciting non-donors, but it is the most efficient. A telephone call from a paid caller to a non-donor or a minimal donor to ask for a gift is less personable because the two parties don't know each other. Sometimes a development director will send out invitations to an event to all donors and prospects without choosing which donors could be interested in the event and those who might not be interested. The response rate might be low to moderate. On a non-profit's website, there may be words and graphics encouraging readers to contribute, but this single message is not personalized. A Facebook post may urge a non-profit's followers to make a charitable gift, but the post is meant for everyone. An email that shares news to non-donors and donors alike may reach everyone on the list, but not everyone will open it or read it.

Personal Approaches to Solicitation of Donors

Development is all about establishing and improving relationships with donors, so setting an appointment with them where they work or where they live to solicit a gift is much more personal and many times more effective. An invitation to a black-tie dinner can be personal, especially when the donor is invited to sit with important administrators, trustees, and the dinner speaker. Enjoying social activities greatly increases the chance that a donor will make a gift because of the relationship the development director has created and nurtured. Speaking with a donor in a setting away from the non-profit is often more effective for soliciting a major gift because the topic of conversation is less about the non-profit and more about the donor. Active listening helps a development director get to know the donor and their families, which is an important step in relationship building. It builds trust and credibility, and both of these virtues are key to making donors comfortable with making major and planned gift decisions.

Effects of Personal and Less Personal Solicitation Methods on Classifications of Donors

High Capacity/Low Interest and Low Capacity/Low Interest

High capacity/low interest: Non-profits must use their finest skills to compete for support from wealthy prospects that don't know who they are. Development officers might assume this type of donor has low interest through conclusions derived from prospect research, but the best kind of prospect research is meeting the donor and learning about their attitudes. The highest-quality kind of invitation by a senior director can eventually bring results.

Low Capacity/low interest: A low capacity rating can be wrong. Prospect research cannot discover all assets or all sources of income. Assuming a prospect has no wealth is short sighted. However, if it's true that their interest is low, then this kind of prospect might be low on a priority list. They can receive periodic mailings and, if there's any interest at all, they won't ask to be taken off the mailing list. Non-profits can take their cues from their requests. In fact, their interest may increase with personal attention from the right staff member.

High Capacity/High Interest and Low Capacity/High Interest

High Capacity/high interest: This type of donor will present themselves often and enthusiastically at special events and other activities that interest them. Personalized solicitation is called for with this donor, and it should be carried out by the staff that know this kind of donor best, including the names and backgrounds of their spouses and children, personal milestones, cultural interests, friends, acquaintances, and also topics to avoid. High capacity/high interest donors are known to come to trust development officers as they would trust their own families.

Low Capacity/high interest: It is tempting to pay attention to prospects with much enthusiasm. They want to engage with the non-profit's employees. Staff should be accommodating, even if they think it's not a good use of time. However, the staff may be surprised if the prospect comes into a large inheritance and notifies the non-profit that it will benefit from a major gift.

Written Messages Used to Reach Donors and Prospects

Annual Fund Donors and Prospects

The conventional wisdom in the direct mail industry is that longer annual fund letters get read more than short ones. It's also true that the more enclosures a non-profit stuff into an envelope, the more curious their readers become. With annual fund prospects and annual fund donors, the direct mail writer should take as many pages as it takes to make their case for support. In the recipient's mind, the longer the letter, the more important the need. Non-profits don't expect recipients to read

51

the whole letter thoroughly, but a reader will scan it and their attention will be drawn to the sentences that are underscored or highlighted. These sentences should be calls to action. The action they want donors to take is go to the website and make a gift, or send a check in the postage-paid envelope.

Planned Giving Donors and Prospects

Longer letters are better than short letters for a planned giving audience. Planned giving donors have made major commitments to the non-profit, and they want to be reassured that they've made the right decision. Pumping them up with good news about the non-profit's results is always a smart approach. Using a planned giving donor to share their story is always interesting. When they talk about their history with the non-profit, what it means to them, and what kind of planned gift they have set up, they are providing testimonials to share with prospects. Planned giving letters should be very light on selling and heavier on information that donors and prospects can use to consider estate gifts. Thinking about making a planned gift can take a lot of thought over a period of years, so any information the letter can provide reinforces the program's advantages. It also helps to repeat the same message in other letters, newsletters, short talks to donors at receptions, at 40th and 50th college reunions for members of the "Golden Circle," in the non-profit's magazine, and on the website.

Written Messages to Inspire Potential Major Gift Donors the Non-profit Doesn't Know

Some non-profits have been very successful working with the media to create stories about their clients to attract the attention of potential donors and inspire them. Philanthropic families have been moved by stories about hardship and the hope a non-profit has given to the less fortunate. They have made generous gifts of cash, stocks, and art to support the mission. In some cases, wealthy donors have donated entire buildings where children without parents can live with supervision from professional social workers. In fact, some donors have contributed buildings and endowments to support their maintenance. Donors who are inspired to give these kinds of generous gifts must work out their anticipated income tax deductions with their attorneys. However, because some attorneys are not entirely familiar with complex charitable giving, it also may be a good idea to include a planned giving director from the non-profit in the gifting process.

Using Oral Communications Techniques to Interest Potential Donors

Development officers can seek out public speaking opportunities in the community to attempt to interest potential donors in their missions. Rotary clubs, church mission committees, women's groups, veterans' associations, mission fairs, church denominational conferences, ethical societies, church congregations, Kiwanis clubs, and other civic groups that are concerned with social welfare issues and social justice can be excellent forums to speak about their missions and the people they help. Members of boards of directors can seek out more speaking opportunities within their social circles to reach groups of potential donors who aren't necessarily members of civic groups. For example, they could invite them to small dinners of friends at their country clubs, to luncheons arranged by women's clubs or men's clubs in churches, and to interested residents of senior living communities and nursing homes. If development officers can collect the names, phone numbers, and email addresses of attendees, they can follow up to try to pique their interest.

Best Practices of Conversation Skills to Solicit Gifts

Development directors can role play with each other to sharpen their conversation skills in order to effectively solicit gifts. For example, it's important not to rush into a solicitation before the prospect is ready. It's also important to not ask a prospect for a gift that's too small. Prospects are hardly ever upset by a solicitation that's too large. Most prospects find it flattering. It's also important to solicit a gift and then not equivocate. The best way to handle this part of the conversation is to let the prospect think about the solicitation and give them time to react. Development directors should not immediately pull back the number and tell the prospect they could give less. If the prospect already has committed a gift to another non-profit, they will tell you. That doesn't mean the answer is "no." It may just mean "not this year." It could mean "yes" later, after the other commitment is fulfilled.

Good Behavioral Habits to Build Solid Relationships with Prospects and Donors

Donors and prospects have to trust a development officer before significant successful solicitations can take place. Experienced development officers learn what qualities make them trustworthy. (1) Don't gossip, especially about other donors or prospects. Donors are aware that development officers meet and spend time with a lot of people and they would not want them gossiping about their own personal lives. In fact, it is a good practice not to discuss anyone else with a donor. (2) If a development officer doesn't know the answer to a donor's question, they should not make it up. Donors and prospects expect the truth from people they trust. It's best to say, "I don't know" and then research it. When a development officer can take time to learn the answer and provide truthful information, they will become credible sources of information in the future. (3) Reserve judgment. A development officer cannot afford to be judgmental about people or decisions made by the administration when they're speaking with donors and prospects. A donor may not have formed opinions yet, or their opinions might differ from the development officer's if they have. It's best not to let opinions drive wedges between development officers and donors.

Lobbing State Legislators on Behalf of Casinos

Some universities and non-profits have solicited businesses like casinos for charitable gifts. A common response from casinos has been a request for a quid pro quo; specifically, casinos typically have asked the non-profits and universities to help them lobby state legislators to relax gambling regulations. It is never legal for non-profits and universities to lobby state legislators on behalf of a casino business. Non-profits keep their 501(c)(3) IRS tax-free designation by agreeing not to advocate for political issues or politicians. It certainly would be illegal and unethical to lobby the legislature on behalf of a highly regulated private business. In the non-profit industry, the organizations that appear to advocate episodically about issues are churches. Specifically, individual Catholic churches have been seen publicly campaigning against abortion laws. Individual evangelical Protestant churches have been seen publicly advocating for conservative politicians. To date the IRS has taken no action against churches that drive this activity; however, other non-profits and universities should not see the IRS's lack of action as carte blanche to become political advocates. Many of them receive revenue from federal contracts, so caution is urged.

Cultivation of Prospects and Donors by CEO or President of Non-profit

The most effective cultivation that ever could occur would be by a president or CEO. Donors and prospects talk to development staff at many events, but a president or CEO wanting to meet them is quite an honor. It's the ultimate honor when a CEO invites them to lunch, to tour the non-profit, to his or her home, and to cultural events. Donors and prospects know the development staff's job is to solicit donors, but a president or CEO has many responsibilities and many demands on his or her time. If the executive has great social skills, which many do, donors and prospects enjoy spending time with him or her because they are interesting people who know many influential people. Cultivation, however, by the CEO always takes place with the assistance and direction from the development vice president who makes sure the CEO is spending time with the donors who can do

53

the non-profit the most good. In that same vein, the development vice president should make sure the CEO isn't spending too much time with people who have no ability to help the non-profit. A CEO who has a socially skilled spouse can engage the finest donors in many social situations. That effort begins with the board. Board members want to be friends with the CEO and his or her spouse, and close friendships can help advance the non-profit in significant ways.

Involving Families in Solicitation of Major and Planned Gifts

Sometimes elderly prospects feel more comfortable when their family members are part of a conversation they have with major and planned giving directors. There are many options that can benefit donors including tax deductions, lifetime income, income streams to the non-profit, income streams to family members, deferred benefits, and other considerations. Donors may decide to leave a specific dollar amount to a charity or a percentage of their assets. It's important to some families and donors to make sure everyone is happy with a gift arrangement so the children and grandchildren don't become resentful and interfere with closing the gift. Adult children and grandchildren may become unhappy with their parent or grandparent giving away what they feel is their inheritance. Children have sued non-profits to have bequests returned to estates. Some of those lawsuits might have been mitigated by conversations between development officers, donors, and their families. They could have been assuaged by directing trust and annuity income to the children for many years and when their parent or grandparent is deceased, the principal is given to the non-profit. Of course, when the family member dies, their descendants will lose the trust and annuity income on which they have relied, also creating possible resentment. However, if a non-profit treats the donor and their family with much consideration and sensitivity, the surviving adult children may make their own charitable gifts to the non-profit in their parent's memory.

Time Spent Soliciting Donors and Prospects

It's a common myth that development officers spend all of their time asking donors for money. In fact, very little time is spent on solicitation. If that were true, there would be very few relationships with donors. Development officers spend most of their time nurturing relationships with donors to build trust and credibility. They are the face of the non-profit, especially when donors haven't connected with anyone else on the staff. When a donor likes the development director and they spend time together, the chances of a donor then making a charitable gift increase. Most gifts happen when the development director asks, but sometimes donors will make a gift without being asked out of affection for the development director. Time spent with donors is more important and more effective than constantly asking for money.

Written Communication Techniques to Solicit Donors and Prospective Donors

Non-profits must word their communications to donors appropriately and tailor their messages to each donor group. A non-profit may write in a casual, lighthearted style to prospects and donors at the base level with premiums like mugs, umbrellas, and t-shirts available for donors that give modestly. These kinds of letters can be mass produced with some personalization, but in general all the wording is the same. When development directors write to donors at the higher levels, they are careful not to mass produce them. When possible, these kinds of letters should be written individually with important and specific details inserted to make them as personal as possible. These letters must contain the donors' exact names and addresses, and nicknames should be used when they are known. In the body of the letter, the amount of their last gift should be dropped in with the date of their last gift. If the development director determines that the donor should be asked for an increased gift, it should be quoted carefully with well-written sentences.

54

Broadening Efforts to Inform Non-Donors and Donors About Charity's Work

Non-profit communications no longer mean just brochures. In order to get donors' attention and provide introductory information about a non-profit, it can't restrict itself only to locations where brochures are displayed. It has to be virtually everywhere. That's why web presence is so important. A non-profit with a top-quality web site can reach potential donors all over the world. However, different generations can be drawn to different kinds of written communications. While older people sometimes have trouble navigating the web, other senior citizens turn to it first. Some individuals become interested when a non-profit is featured in publications that interest them. Others may pay attention to an article in their church bulletin about a non-profit and they may assume their church endorses it. Other non-profits can seek publicity in magazines that are targeted to wealthy individuals, senior citizens, high-end products, people who travel, and others that have generous disposable income.

Active Listening

While many people think of themselves as active listeners, many people have never developed good listening skills. In fundraising, development officers must learn to be active listeners if their goal is to convey to donors that their opinions, suggestions, and complaints are heard and understood. This is important because donors become emotionally attached to a non-profit, and it's important to them to engage in discussions about the organization's activities. In some cases, donors and development officers become good friends and it's important to nurture these kinds of friendships with active listening. What listening behavior should development officers learn? (1) Listen without interrupting. (2) Listen without waiting to jump in and offer their own opinions and experiences. (3) Don't be distracted by other people or background events. (4) Maintain eye contact with the donor who is speaking. (5) Nod at intervals to show understanding. (6) Let the donor know they're interesting by using the words "yes" and "go on." (7) Wait until the donor is finished talking before asking questions and do so without communicating judgment.

Office Setting and Assisted Living or Skilled Nursing Facilities

When listening to a donor in their office setting, it's important to gauge how much time they will give you and direct your conversation accordingly. Often a donor will welcome a development director into their office, and then tell their assistant that the appointment will wrap up in 10 minutes. Sometimes that's a signal for the assistant to interrupt after 10 minutes to end the appointment. It's also a signal to the development director that their time is limited. When this is the case, the development officer should direct the conversation to get what they came for, whether it's a solicitation, an invitation to become involved, or advice about prospects. In the case of a donor living in a facility, it's very important to carve out a lot of time for the visit. Elderly donors enjoy long visits. They like having time to talk about themselves, their families, their careers, and their involvement with the non-profit's early days. It's important to remember that when an elderly donor is visited, the conversation could easily be the only one they have that day. It also could be the longest conversation they have all week or all month. Donors value the time spent with someone from the non-profit, particularly if they're not asked for money every time they meet. It's common for elderly donors to care about development officers as they would members of their own families. Planned gifts often develop from these relationships, sometimes without being asked.

Careful Listening

Discretion with Call Reports

A professional development officer will visit a donor or prospect, listen carefully, and remember important things about their conversation. Development officers should never make notes during a conversation with a prospect or a donor. It makes them nervous, self-conscious, suspicious, and can ruin any more attempts to interview them for more information. The better method is to make notes quickly after the visit is over, and to make sure the important details are accurate. When they return to the office, the development director can create a formal call report in the system. The call report should include the name, address, phone number, email address, Facebook page name, Twitter handle, and fax number of the prospect or donor and this information should be checked against the data in the system. It's up to the development director to change the donor's record in the system because no one else on the staff knows what is new. Then the development director should write everything they learned during the appointment. However, it is very important for anyone who writes a call report to be discreet. Call report writers should write about the facts and not speculate about what may or may not be true. For example, development directors should never write about hunches they have, such as a person's sexual identification, the meaning of conflicts within the family, and the person's IQ or emotional intelligence. If the development director guesses about very personal narratives, these comments will remain in the file for many years, and if enough people read them, they will become facts.

Community Members

During special events, members of the community may approach the non-profit's employees and start conversations about their beliefs in the organization and its clients. It's important for the employees to listen very carefully for errors, misunderstandings, complaints, and outdated information. Community members may complain about the charity operating an orphanage in their backyards, when in fact it hasn't operated an orphanage for decades. Or they may be in a mood to tell the non-profit how they feel about the religious organization that runs it, again when the charity hasn't been affiliated for many years. At a small college gathering, community members might ask if it still offers college courses that have become irrelevant and have not been in the course catalog since anyone can remember. The non-profit staff can take these encounters back to the public relations or marketing department that can decide how it may create its messages to reflect contemporary services and clients. Correcting false assumptions can change donors' minds, but only after the messages have time to sink in.

Problem with Solely Relying on Software Screening

Almost always, prospect-searching software will identify individuals in the non-profit's database that have high salaries. It will give them very high ratings and development directors will focus on them. When a potential prospect is the president of a hospital, a social services agency, a university, or a nationally known non-profit, it is tempting for a development director to look up their salaries. It seems to be a relevant assumption at the time that these prospects are capable of major gifts for any non-profit that interests. They may be capable, but experience should tell a development director that they are not likely to commit to any non-profit but their own. The vast majority of well-paid non-profit leaders give generously to their own organizations but not to others. This is one reason why the best prospect research can be a conversation with a prospect to discover their interests. A non-profit leader will quickly reveal that the board of directors, major donors, and staff look to the president to lead by example in personal philanthropy. If a president makes a large gift to a different non-profit, it sends a signal to the community that their own organization isn't worth supporting. The best practice is to rule out leaders of other any other non-profits and code them as non-prospects accordingly in the database.

Importance of Nonverbal Communication When Listening to Donors

While people know they're being listened to when they speak without being interrupted or judged, they also are intuitive about the physical behavior of the listener. For example, noticing body language is common, especially if the effect is negative. Listeners should not glance at their smartphones during conversations or the donor will think what they say is not interesting. Other distractions that hinder active listening can be glancing at sports on television screens, looking around the room, glancing at other people, and speaking to other people while the donor is speaking. Active listeners can lean toward the speaker, turn toward them, uncross their arms, and mirror the speaker's posture. Mirroring means placing their hands and arms and tilting their head in the same way as the donor and matching their volume. Above all, maintain eye contact.

Team Building

The conventional wisdom about team building is that a group of people working for the same mission could benefit by going through exercises that help reveal individual strengths and build trust. Theoretically, a team-building workshop can reduce or eliminate resentments, anger, and personality conflicts between individuals. Frequently, the effects are short lived. The real work goes beyond performing exercises and using this time to get to the root of the problems. If a board of directors is in constant conflict, maybe the root cause is the members don't understand what is expected of them. If board roles aren't clear, members can become frustrated and take it out on each other. The same circumstance can apply to staff. Using team-building time to discover the larger issues at hand can bring important frustrations to light, like lack of leadership, poor planning, or leaders and staff that don't buy into a plan.

Trust Building in an Organization

Trust comes from the top down. Staff look to their department leader to set standards for how everyone will behave. If the department head has integrity, speaks honestly, does not blame individuals for mistakes, works harder than the staff, and accomplishes more than everyone else, they will become someone everyone can respect as a leader. If a leader can discourage negative behaviors like gossiping, oppositional defiance, undermining other people, duplicity, and lying to hide errors, the staff will understand what is not acceptable. Just as important is to treat staff like the real people they are and not as mere functions. When a leader takes a sincere interest in the life of a direct report, they convey the person's value as a human being. Taking staff out to lunch or coffee and asking them to share personal stories can bond better by treating them as friends. When employees feel the boss's honest interest and concern, loyalty builds and remains as long as the behavior is consistent. An employee who feels valued is more likely to feel that others have relevant things to contribute. Trust is built over time with uninterrupted behavior modeling by senior administrators.

Corporations' Spheres of Influences on Non-profits

Corporations, depending on the size of the support they give to non-profits, may vault charities into national recognition. This can happen when corporations sponsor television programs on PBS, for example, and use non-profits' names and logos to show their partnerships. The public may begin seeing a non-profit's logo and name more often as programs appear more frequently. It may take years for the general public to register the non-profit's name and logo, but the image may finally stick with many viewers for years to come. Special events for non-profits also may carry the logos of corporate sponsors prominently. To some observers, this association makes a very good impression and can create an image of the non-profit as large, healthy, and legitimate. Conversely, donors may stop giving to the non-profit at the first sign of a corporate logo because they feel their contributions are unneeded.

Governmental Spheres of Influences on Non-profits

Non-profits are regulated by the states in which they operate, and these regulations may be light or onerous. Some non-profits that operate with state contracts have to provide regular reports on their activities to state governments. In some cases, the governmental bodies will require proof of their accreditation. Politics can impact non-profits, especially when political parties in power push a wedge issue into local and national campaigns. Non-profits like Planned Parenthood, the International Rescue committee that helps immigrants, and wealthy private universities with large endowments have been challenged by politicians that seek to make them targets for controversy. For example, grassroots political movements can force state legislators to reverse laws intended to reduce or eliminate harm to living creatures—laws that have been passed at the urging of non-profit groups. Tight regulations on planned giving vehicles can make it very difficult to operate estate giving programs in some states.

Spheres of Influences on Non-profits

Social

The social spheres of influence are very important to non-profits. When people who are respected and admired become supporters of specific charities, they can make all the difference in the world. Wealthy celebrities that decide to support rescue and rebuilding efforts after a natural disaster can influence countless others to donate their time and money to help the victims. This also is true for famous people who give to and promote non-profits very visibly to a national audience. Cultural non-profits like symphonies and art museums may gain the interest of very wealthy people who maintain their financial support for many years, and their friends and admirers will do so too. In some families, younger generations will contribute to non-profits because the older generations did, and the older relatives made a big impression on them. It can become a tradition. To demonstrate their friendships, some individuals give to each other's charities and attend their special events.

Legal Profession

The legal profession can influence non-profits when tax and estate-planning attorneys hold events for mutually beneficial purposes. A non-profit may hold an estate-planning event for the public with the sponsorship of a law firm. The public may attend because the law firm's sponsorship makes the event credible and attendees, as a side benefit, will learn about the non-profit at the event. This sponsorship may enable non-profits to hold more frequent events to raise their visibility and to scout for new prospects among the attendees.

Insurance Industry

The life insurance industry markets life insurance policies as forms of planned gifts. The donor takes out a life insurance policy and designates the non-profit as the beneficiary. If the donor makes the annual premium payments to the non-profit, which then sends them to the insurance company, those premium payments are tax deductible. Does the non-profit recognize a life insurance policy as a planned gift? It might, but it probably will not count it as revenue that will be received in the future because donors can change the beneficiaries at any time. If a donor runs short of cash, they may ask the non-profit to take over the premium payments on their life insurance policy. What should the non-profit do? If the charity makes the premium payments on a life insurance policy gift, it is paying for a gift to itself. The best answer is to decline. A board may decide to pay the premiums on a case-by-case basis, but it should not become a common practice. Other life insurance donors may ask for the same favor.

Medical Profession

The medical profession may refer patients to non-profits that use support groups that can help care for them emotionally and spiritually during and after the treatment of their diseases. Doctors encounter patients daily who cannot afford medical care, and the doctors will turn to non-profit clinics to treat patients with long-term disease and chronic conditions. Some hospitals operate a "mini medical school" for patients to learn more about wellness and how advanced medicine has become. Doctors will lecture the classes and plenty of time is left for questions and answers. Mini med schools attract a large percentage of older patients who are concerned about becoming sick and dying. If they feel comforted, optimistic, informed, and empowered by what they have learned in a specific hospital, they're more likely to choose it for treatments.

Religion

The Catholic Church had and continues to have a large role in serving people through its non-profit work. It runs hospitals, universities, and social services agencies across the United States. The mission of Catholic non-profits is to serve everyone in need regardless of their race, ethnicity, social standing, or beliefs. Jewish congregations can encourage their members to fundraise for Israeli non-profits. The Church of Jesus Christ of Latter-day Saints encourages tithing. Protestant churches vote to support missions in the United States and overseas.

Board of Directors

The board of directors' largest influence will be, and should be, on the CEO. A board that stands behind its CEO gives them confidence, the freedom to try new things, the freedom to fail, and teaches them new skills will nurture a CEO and help them grow. Board members can introduce the CEO, particularly if they are new, to experts in the non-profit's field to give them someone to mentor them. Board members can also help the CEO and the non-profit financially by finding major gifts in the community. Major gifts may come from the board members' friends and colleagues and they may be significant enough to construct large buildings according to a strategic plan. Board members also can provide testimonials to potential funders that want reassurance about the non-profit's viability. These testimonials can basically guarantee that the non-profit will be around for the long term and it will use the major gifts according to the donor's intent.

Other Non-profits

Smart non-profits create alliances to help each other. Small non-profits sometimes bind together in an alliance to push for legislative changes that will benefit them and their clients. Often, social services non-profits share resources like computer servers, physicians, training, and clergy. Non-profit alliances work on lobbying state governments for better contract terms such as more funding for client services and increased day rates for residents. Larger non-profits have been known to help smaller organizations out financially with lines of credit, loans, and loaned executives. Wealthy churches support non-profits financially.

Building Constituencies

Non-profits can increase their profile in the community they serve by inviting natural constituents to join an advisory board. A natural constituent is someone who has a strong interest in the non-profit but who may not yet be board material. A constituent can be invited to join an advisory board by the president or CEO with staff laying the groundwork before the request is made. Constituents are flattered to be invited, eager to help, and they often expect to be solicited for a gift in order to join. When advisory boards meet, the president or CEO can speak at the meeting and share some insider information. Feeling like an insider is a very effective cultivation tool and it's likely to help inspire an advisory board member to give more. A deeper understanding of a non-profit's needs also can equip members to share the information with their friends and family that may become donors.

Encouraging Constituencies to Optimize Relationships with Each Other

A board of trustees is a constituency that may or may not be aware of the other important constituencies in and around a non-profit, but the staff members who see links can encourage the groups to work together. A volunteer fundraising committee that works on raising annual fund gifts can work with the board's development committee to exchange prospect and donor names and assign the ones each individual feels confident about. A board member could create a challenge grant and communicate it to both committees to spread word of the opportunity. The officers of a 50th reunion committee at a college could work with the legacy society to offer the names of people who might be good prospects for planned gifts. The admissions office can forward the names and occupations of parents of current students to development officers to research and discover new prospects. The alumni relations staff also can forward names to the development office when they spot good prospects.

Engaging a Prospect with a University

At a university, an alumna can be engaged by asking them to help out by getting involved in reunion planning. If they are interested, they can connect with their classmates and notify them of the reunion weekend dates. This planning should begin a year before the event. The alumna can be asked to form a planning committee, and presumably they will invite people they know to join. Reunion planning committees will stimulate the members to stir up nostalgia about their days together on campus. With these conversations, they will begin to hold the university in higher esteem. So, the programs within "alumni relations" really are all about development and bringing alumni back to reconnect with the long-range purpose of cultivating gifts.

Leading a Newly Involved Prospect to the Next Level

If the aforementioned alumna has had a good experience running a reunion, the development officer could make a note to re-contact the individual in four years to ask them to chair the gift committee for their next milestone reunion. While some alumnae will shy away from soliciting their classmates, others might accept for two reasons: (1) reconnecting with their friends and (2) they see a compelling purpose for raising a reunion class gift. The funds might be used for a scholarship, for example. Chairing a gift committee can engage them on a deeper level with their classmates because fundraising is always personal. It also can engage them more deeply with the development officer because gift committee work is complex, and the solicitation work needs professional support. Once the gift committee has been successful raising money for a scholarship, the alumnae will feel confident that they can help in other ways. They may wait to be asked, or they may ask for a new assignment.

Making Donors Feel They're Accomplishing Something Very Important to the Non-profit

A development officer can invite a donor at the $1,000 level to chair a fundraising committee to cultivate and solicit identified prospects for new $1,000 gifts. It's an honor and it can be intimidating, but committed donors will at least give it a chance. At this level, the development officer will be sharing prospect information with the fundraising chair and their committee. It's important not to give the chair too much information about their prospects or they can easily feel that they are invading the privacy of others. It's also important not to let the chair know too much because the chair will wonder what the non-profit knows about them. Prospect research can reach deeply into donors' and prospects' lives, and the development officer should be the model of discretion. Theoretically, the development officer should give the chair and their committee members some prospects they can have success with soliciting. The concept of making the volunteers feel proud of their work is an important one, but not often easy to carry out. Development officers can go with the volunteers to solicitation appointments and, when the volunteer falters, the development officer can close the ask. This kind of relationship can build more trust between the development officer and the chair.

Effect of Nominating a Donor to the Board of Trustees

When a donor is nominated to the non-profit's board of trustees, it's both an honor and a time to pause. Most donors will ask right away how much of a financial commitment they will have to make. A crucial mistake that a development officer can often make at this point is to be vague. Sometimes non-profit staff and CEOs are so hopeful that the donor will accept that they tell them they don't have to commit. When it comes to giving records, 100% of the trustees should be giving. The development officer or the CEO should solicit new trustees for major gifts because as trustees they have a fiduciary responsibility to the non-profit. Assuming they can and do make major gifts, the donors will feel exceptionally important to the non-profit—at first. Afterward, it's up to the CEO to involve them in meaningful ways or they will resign, feeling their roles weren't important. Cultivation doesn't end when the donor says yes. It is continuous.

Fundraising and Philanthropy

In short, fundraising is an emotionally motivated effort to solve an immediate problem. Fundraising, for example, occurs when donors give money to the American Red Cross during a natural disaster, or when family and friends set up a Go Fund Me page to help a patient pay for medical bills. Fundraising is conducted on a short-term basis to address a crisis. Philanthropy is a long-term, sustained effort to improve conditions and to build up programs and structures to prevent crises. Giving starving people fish to eat is fundraising. Teaching them how to fish is philanthropy.

Fundraising Programs in the Past

The Catholic Church actually started the charitable gift annuity concept several centuries ago in Europe. The Catholic Church offered people income for life if they would donate large assets to the church. People would be paid income until their deaths, at which time the church would own the residuum. When the bubonic plague shortened many peoples' lives, the church acquired residuum earlier and larger than normal. Charitable gift annuities were used in the 1700s by the Presbyterian Church to provide for retired ministers, widows, and orphans. In the 20th century, individuals have bought annuities to provide them with stable, consistent income when the markets have been too unreliable for some investors. In other words, fundraising has attracted individuals from the beginning by offering them some benefits in return. Altruism has not been as self-sacrificing as some of us have been led to believe through historical narratives or family anecdotes.

Philanthropy in the Past

Philanthropy, rather than working on the ground by taking in assets and giving income, began functioning on a philosophical level with Andrew Carnegie and John D. Rockefeller. Carnegie set up a foundation for the long-term improvement of public health and public education. Rockefeller founded the University of Chicago where he could fund research in science and use the research to inform teaching in the classrooms. Rockefeller's contribution to higher education raised the bar of what can be accomplished with major backing. His philanthropy didn't necessarily address destruction left by a natural disaster, or rescue families from the deplorable conditions of poverty.

Like Carnegie, Rockefeller made the world a better place from a deep and lengthy commitment to improving the human condition.

Fundraising Today and the Last Several Decades

the 1950s, mothers volunteered for the March of Dimes in their neighborhoods when they solicited gifts door to door from their friends and neighbors. Volunteer captains organized groups to solicit door-to-door for the American Cancer Society. The donations were small, but taken together, the cash from these campaigns added up and provided helpful revenue, especially since no labor costs were involved. Mothers participate in school bake sales, Girl Scouts sell cookies, Boy Scouts collect canned goods, Cub Scouts sell popcorn, and other organizations sell entertainment coupon books. Raffles continue to be popular, and trivia nights have grown exponentially. Veterans still sell candy bars outside grocery stores in temperate weather, followed by Salvation Army bell ringers in all kinds of weather. High school kids wash cars for donations. All of these activities generate immediate cash, and volunteer solicitors that handle money can feel immediate gratification from their work. However, these kinds of sporadic donations don't always sustain large organizations for very long. That's why large organizations put most of their efforts into development or philanthropy.

Philanthropy Today

Today, non-profits are benefitting from immense wealth built through the marketing and sales of new technology, stock market investments, excellent returns from real estate sales, and international trade. Individuals and corporations seek help from philanthropic advisors to form charitable foundations to benefit deserving charities. They want to analyze how well non-profits perform as they carry out their missions. They seek out seats on boards of charities to become involved in improving elementary education, healthcare, higher education, and outreach to impoverished Third World countries. Today's philanthropists are more concerned with sustaining non-profits over the long term and less with giving money to solve immediate problems. Part of what motivates them is leaving their legacy by helping to effect permanent positive change. They also are motivated by the tax deductions they can take advantage of, but most development professionals will offer the wisdom that most individuals do not give charitable donations because of tax benefits. Beyond sustaining non-profits during their lifetimes, today's philanthropists create foundations to maintain charitable support long after they are deceased.

Benefits of Fundraising Programs

Annual Fund

Virtually no non-profit can sustain itself or plan on a solid future without development. Even if a non-profit has contracts from the state, any contract can be abrogated. Non-profits need a continuous flow of cash to help pay for operations expenses, including payroll, utilities, and insurance. They can't afford to run short on cash. The annual fund provides unrestricted revenue for the non-profit so it can use the donations wherever they are needed. The annual fund runs all year long, so a non-profit doesn't have to wait months to receive funds. Gifts from the annual fund are unpredictable, however, and the gifts will come according to each donor's schedule. In some months, the cash flow will be a trickle and then, in November and December, it can be heavy. To cover expenses during low-cash months, a non-profit can draw income from their endowment. Large, healthy endowments with liquid assets can be an essential backup any time cash is low. Assets invested outside the endowment can also help.

Planned Giving

Specifically, a planned giving program can deliver very generous bequests to a non-profit regularly if the development office has been cultivating and soliciting donors for decades. Bequests in the six-figure range can be very helpful when non-profits face deficits and cash flow problems. In fact, some non-profits calculate the average bequest that comes in every year and budget for them as revenue that can be relied on. In 2014, total bequests received by non-profits totaled $28.13 billion. Planned giving alone might fix some temporary shortages; however, bequests are almost always surprises. When a donor notifies the non-profit that they have included a bequest for it in their wills and they reveal the amount, the non-profit records what is called a bequest expectancy. This is an attempt to project how much money the bequest will be when it is received some years in the future.

Corporate and Foundation

Corporate and foundation fundraising programs can help non-profits pay for programs that benefit the donor and the recipient. However, they don't pay for unrestricted operating funds. Foundations, for the most part, are interested in funding programs that have a specific purpose with outcomes that can be measured and evaluated. They don't help boost the size of operational accounts because most foundations don't like to pay for overhead. Non-profits basically cannot count on receiving a foundation grant or a corporate gift at specific times of the year because they make awards on their own schedules. Once a foundation has made a grant and a non-profit has done a good job of reporting results, it may be able to rely on receiving the grant for several years. However, a non-profit that fails to send timely and complete reports of how the grant was used and what the outcomes were may not receive it again.

Using Benefits of Membership as Incentives for Prospects to Join or Members to Renew

The use of member benefits seems to be steady across most of the non-profit universe. Non-profits that have very diverse constituencies can use a sliding scale of rewards to incentivize members to increase their payments. Botanical gardens, libraries, and museums have a wide range of people who are members, so offering a variety of benefits seems to be standard procedure. Often a matrix is used to display how rewards build as a member gives more. These incentives begin with premiums like tote bags and umbrellas and increase to offers of free tickets to the non-profit's events, special preview nights of new exhibits, tours, discounts in the gift shop, and exclusive private lunch meetings with the CEO. However, membership has its limits. A non-profit may find it difficult to persuade members to move up from paying basic membership fees to making outright charitable gifts. The price is higher, and perhaps the benefits are not that much better than membership benefits. Many universities have closed their alumni association dues or membership fees because alumni will remain stuck at the same contribution levels for years, and they don't see a reason to send in anything but a membership check.

Using Premiums to Acquire New Donors and Retain Existing Donors

A premium is considered a gift to a donor in return for their charitable contribution. Charities offer premiums to motivate prospects to give for the first time. Common premiums include coffee mugs, umbrellas, tote bags, and t-shirts. Some donors will make charitable gifts because they like the premiums. Non-profits also use premiums to motivate donors to increase their giving. Usually, a non-profit will ask donors to move up to a new giving club in order to receive the premium. Donors may be motivated to increase their gifts to join a higher giving club for the prestige. Non-profits frequently name their giving clubs for their founders. Giving clubs are most effective at the entry level ($100) and at the highest level ($1,000). Charities are restricted by the IRS to keep the value of

Copyright © Mometrix Media. You have been licensed one copy of this document for personal use only. Any other reproduction or redistribution is strictly prohibited. All rights reserved.

premiums at or below $65. If a charity provides a donor with a gift that exceeds this amount, it must deduct the difference from the value of the donor's gift.

Offering Naming Rights to Motivate Donors

Perhaps the highest honor a donor can receive is a building named for them. Building names can live in perpetuity, long after the donor is deceased. Donors also enjoy naming buildings that mean something important to them. A donor whose life has been saved by a medical team might most enjoy naming a cardiac unit, for example. An alumnus of a university may name a scholarship in honor of their favorite professor, perhaps the professor that helped them to become successful. The cost of naming rights varies from institution to institution, and from large to small opportunities. At larger universities, a named scholarship might have a price tag of $50,000 or more. A large medical center may set $5 million as a minimum amount a donor has to give to name a hospital. Smaller independent schools might only require $10,000 to name a classroom.

Consistent Naming Rights Policy

In order for the donor and prospect community to develop long-term respect for an institution, non-profits should create strict standards for naming rights and stick to them.

For example, if a university's requirement is a $5 million gift to name a building, it should not waver from this minimum under pressure. A board member may bring in a capital donor who would give $1 million if the university will name a building for them. The university should stick to its $5 million minimum and not give the rights away for less. If donors and prospects begin to talk about "deals" the university makes for capital gifts, the honor of a naming right will lose its luster. The university also risks damage to its image if the community thinks it is desperate for money. Standards are important for a current capital campaign and future campaigns.

Giving Clubs

Giving clubs are all about recognition. The more money a donor gives, the more prominently their name will appear on the honor roll. Traditionally, the names of the largest donors appear first and toward the top of the page. Many non-profits name their giving clubs after their founders or other giants in the history of the organization, with the most prestigious names assigned to top donor clubs. Usually, the donor clubs end at or about the $100 donation level. In telemarketing and in direct mail, some non-profits will ask small donors to join a giving club. When they communicate with existing club members, they will ask them to move up to a higher club level for more visibility and, in some cases, more benefits. Sometimes the benefits at higher club levels include lunch with the CEO, premiums that become more expensive as donors give more, invitations to special exhibits the day before they open to the general public, guided tours, galas for members and prospective members, special parking passes, and signed books.

Challenge Grant

To acquire new donors, non-profits often use challenge grants to capture the attention of non-donors and motivate them to begin giving by explaining how their gifts will be doubled. A non-profit may promote a new challenge grant by telling its audience that a specific couple will "match every new gift" that's donated during the current campaign. Non-donors are told that their gift will be doubled by the challengers. To give the offer more urgency, non-profits often say that the couple will match all new gifts only after a goal for new gifts has been met. Or they will say that the gifts will be matched only if they are made within a specific time period. Non-profits, however, should be cautioned about how much urgency and drama they attach to the matching theme because most

64

challengers have either already committed to giving the full amount and they will match outside the so-called limited time period as well. There is virtually no chance the challenge will fail.

Telemarketing Pledge

A pledge can be relatively small when it's collected during telemarketing. After the telemarketing night is over, callers will write down the pledges they have collected. A small package with the pledge amount filled in on a card will be sent with a return envelope. The development director periodically runs reports that show unpaid pledges to date. Reminders will be sent. Every two months, more reports are run to show unpaid pledges and reminders are mailed again. As the end of the year nears, development directors often have to put callers back on the phones to call individuals who still haven't fulfilled their pledges. It can be expensive and time consuming to put this effort into the collection of pledges, but it is worth the effort. A rule of thumb says that if a non-profit can call in 85% of its pledges, it is doing well. Unfortunately, some non-profits don't pay close attention to unpaid pledges and a considerable amount of gift revenue gets left on the table.

Major Gift Pledge

Development directors work hard to move donors from annual fund levels of $1,000 and less to $5,000, $10,000, and more, depending on what a non-profit considers a major gift. At some universities, museums, and symphonies, a major gift is $100,000. It may take several years to move a donor up to the major gift pledge, and when donors agree to the amount, it's optimal to get their pledge in writing. Some donors ask for between three to five years to pay it off. Non-profits have to make their own decisions about how long they will extend payments, but a rule of thumb is that five years is too long. Donors get payment fatigue. What seemed like a noble and exciting commitment turns into what feels like paying bills on an installment plan. It's not uncommon for people who pledge to stop paying after two or three years because they've become bored or another charity has piqued their interest or both. Development directors can meet with donors privately and gently remind them of their pledges, but these nudges should be followed up with written requests for pledge fulfillment.

Making Donations at the End of December

Almost all donors who use credit cards to make charitable gifts use the non-profit's website. Donors know that they must make their online credit card gifts by December 31 to get credited for a tax-deductible donation. Before the web enabled them to go online to use a charity's giving page, everyone mailed in their MasterCard or Visa card numbers. Some donors still send in gift envelopes and they write their credit card numbers inside the envelope. What many do not understand is if they mail in their credit card numbers on December 31, they will not receive a tax-deduction for that year because the charity did not open the gift envelope and charge the card until after January 1. The IRS rule is that the donor takes the deduction for the gift in the year their card is charged, not when it is mailed. Some donors call their charities and ask them to change the date the card is charged so they can receive credit for the preceding years. A gift acceptance policy approved by the non-profit will protect development officers from being bullied by giving them a rule to use with the donor about why this cannot be done.

Admitting to Mistakes and Returning Donors' Money

The best qualities a development officer can project are honestly and integrity. Development officers who are consistently honest and who can admit mistakes—and fix them promptly—are highly respected by the donor community. For example, a medium-sized non-profit successfully solicited a religious order for a large grant to support the salaries of new in-home therapists for

65

in foster care. Inside the non-profit, several supervisors changed jobs, resigned, or were ...ned and new supervisors knew nothing of the grant. At the end of the fiscal year, only half of ...ant money had been spent. The non-profit contacted the religious order, admitted the error, apologized, and explained the circumstances, and gave back the money it didn't spend. The order gave the non-profit a new grant the following year. More than 20 years ago, Greenpeace was sued in a European court, and the non-profit appealed to its donors for funds to pay their legal bills. When the case ended, the judge did not hold Greenpeace responsible for their legal costs. Greenpeace wrote to its donors and offered to refund every gift that was sent to help them pay their legal bills. Most of the donors allowed Greenpeace to keep the money and use it for other purposes.

Donor Requesting a Refund

A donor requesting a refund doesn't happen often, but when it does, the non-profit should be aware that a charitable gift is irrevocable and that the charity has no obligation to return it. A development officer ought to be able to refer to the organization's gift acceptance policies to enable them to respond with the language approved by the board. There may be some significant scenarios: (1) The donor may have sent in a check, received an acknowledgment letter, and now wants the money returned so he can take the tax deduction and not spend any money. (2) The donor's employer may already have matched his gift. If that has occurred, does the non-profit return the matching gift? (3) There may have been tax credits available and they may have been awarded to the donor. Does the non-profit report this to the agency that issued the tax credits? Does it ask the donor to return them? What if the donor has already used his tax credits? Again, a gift acceptance policy will relieve the development officer of formulating an awkward decision that someone might dispute.

Revocable and Irrevocable Planned Gifts

A bequest is a paragraph in a will that directs the executor to contribute a percentage or fixed amount of the decedent's assets. It is revocable at any time. A donor might direct their attorney to add bequests to other non-profits or completely delete another non-profit from the bequest. This is the reason most non-profits do not count on bequests when they plan a campaign. Another gift in this category is the revocable living trust. However, a charitable gift annuity is irrevocable. This requirement is based on the fact that the non-profit pays income to the donor for life in exchange for receiving the assets from the annuity upon the donor's death. A charitable remainder trust is irrevocable because the donor has promised that a charity will receive the remainder of the assets when the trust ends. A non-profit might recognize donors publicly who have declared that the non-profit is in their wills or trusts. Non-profits also may recognize deceased donors who have made gifts from their estates after their deaths. All of them can be listed as members of a legacy society.

Stewardship

Stewardship means publicly acknowledging a donor's importance to a non-profit so the donor will feel appreciated and will remain involved. If they remained involved and the stewardship is high quality and consistent, the donor is more likely to give again. The highest honor for a donor is to have a non-profit name a building or a wing in their name. Major donors also appreciate awards and awards dinners to honor them, scholarships named for them, honorary degrees, invitations to speak at events, opportunities to chair campaigns, election to the board of trustees, and requests to represent a university at another university's commencement ceremonies. Some universities have stewardship coordinators on staff to create calendars for each major donor. They remind development directors of donors' birthdays, their children's graduation dates, their grandchildren's birthdays, and other important dates. More common ways to honor moderate-level donors include inscribing their names on bricks, putting their names on group plaques, printing their giving levels

in an honor roll of donors, inviting them to events honoring their club-level giving, introducing them to people the non-profit serves, and asking them to chair or participate in special initiatives.

Impact Reporting

The millennial generation and Gen X populations generally expect more than traditional stewardship from a non-profit. When they contribute, they want to know how their money is being used. Reading about concrete uses of their donations enables them to judge how money is flowing through the non-profit to the people who need it, and how productively it is being used. Millennials and Gen Xers often have many questions about a non-profit's financials, and development directors should be prepared to answer them. Millennials and Gen Xers don't fit into traditional demographic groups of major donors because many of them have not reached their peak income decade, but someday, if they do, they will remember the non-profits that were responsive with relevant information. Also, non-profits that are awarded grants are expected to do impact reporting to foundations. Generally, this kind of impact reporting is more technical because program officers at foundations are experts in their fields and they request very specific reporting that may take the form of statistics.

Relationship Building

Using Social Media

Non-profits generally have been slower to use the full potential of social media than the corporate private sector. For the most part, non-profits use Facebook and Twitter to communicate with their followers because it's (1) free and (2) easy to use and widely acceptable. The problems non-profits have is (1) not enough staff to communicate to their followers frequently enough on a consistent basis and (2) not enough money to pay staff to design social media vehicles that can compete for viewers' attention successfully. Marketing departments or development staff frequently try to produce social media messages, but they often don't have real web expertise. Non-profits can concentrate their efforts on using social media to communicate with the segments of their followers they care about messaging most.

Using Email

Using email to communicate with interested constituents is used heavily by political, retail, and entertainment organizations. The non-profit community was relatively late getting into emailing donors and prospects, and sometimes non-profits don't execute it well. It's not unusual for non-profit email to be automatically diverted to a junk mail folder. Donors and prospects receive junk mail every day and it's easy to make a snap judgment to ignore any email that looks like it will try convincing someone to buy a product or service. Non-profit emails must be created to stand out, to get the donor's attention, and to get donors to read it. Non-profits also must vary their emails. Some of them could tell stories about the people they serve with excellent photos. Others could inform donors about impending political action that could threaten the non-profit's survival. These emails should call the recipient to action and make a gift right away online. The wrong kinds of emails can turn donors off, cause them to lose interest, and unsubscribe. Non-profits need email experts that can do the messaging correctly.

Culture of Philanthropy

A culture of philanthropy means that everyone inside the non-profit is aware of how their behavior affects donors' and prospective donors' opinions of the organization and, ultimately, the non-profit's ability to raise funds. While it's important to pay attention to the program and the clients it serves, it's also vital for employees to examine what they say and how they say it when they are

67

talking with the general public. If members of the board of directors don't speak positively and effectively about the non-profit, the development director will have a very difficult time raising funds. Employees with extensive social networks can create negative impressions about their employers if they complain to their friends about their problems on the job. A receptionist who is positive and helpful to a donor raises the donor's opinion of the non-profit, but a receptionist who is rude to a donor can ruin the relationship between the donor and the non-profit. When a development director is working on a grant application, the finance and program staffs have to be on board and supply needed information. Staff that balk at helping development make it difficult to receive foundation funding that will help everyone. Everyone is an ambassador. Developing and maintaining a culture of philanthropy starts and is maintained at the top.

Volunteer Involvement

Productive Volunteer Personality Types and Attributes

When a non-profit is looking for volunteers, it is important to fit the right person into the job. Extroverts can make excellent organizers for fun runs, galas, reunions, auctions, trivia nights, and other events. Introverts can help scanning lists, assembling mailing packets, researching new addresses and phone numbers, and other detailed work. Volunteers will interact with a non-profit's internal and external audiences, so using some discretion when involving them is important. Volunteers must be discreet about their opinions of the non-profit's work, they must not gossip about other volunteers or full-time employees, and they may not share information about clients. Development directors normally deal with projects that contain a lot of volume, so it's important to involve volunteers who will accomplish a great deal of work. The non-profit has to be able to count on their participation on a regular schedule.

Volunteers

Non-profits can use volunteers to do many tasks. Volunteer involvement cultivates individuals for annual gifts and major gifts in the future. Volunteers become more invested in the mission the more hours they give and that investment frequently turns into commitment. That commitment can and does stimulate bequests. When non-profits begin to think about volunteer assignments, first they must evaluate the abilities and professional skills of each volunteer. There's an axiom many senior development directors repeat: Don't ask a retired CEO to lick envelopes. A non-profit must use a volunteer's abilities intelligently or they will lose the volunteer. Someone who doesn't want to commit too much time and who doesn't want to get deep into details may be perfect for assembling direct mail packages and sending out pledge reminders. A university president might be ideal to chair a non-profit board's finance committee for a period of years. Outgoing individuals who have positive opinions about the non-profit can be appointed as ambassadors to speak enthusiastically among their social circles. Volunteers who are noticed by staff may stimulate prospect research that reveals some promising background factors. Staff may look at these volunteers as prospects for advisory board or board of directors' memberships.

Volunteer Role Descriptions

Every volunteer appreciates having a job description. When expectations are clear, volunteers can decide if the time required, the skill level, and the role is right for them. Most volunteers do not want to get in over their heads with assignments for which they have no experience or aptitude. Once they agree on their assignments, volunteers can feel confident in moving ahead with their work. When they become involved in their assigned tasks, volunteers may offer to do more, or they may decide they want to do less and their job descriptions should be adjusted for their comfort level. Volunteers who raise money for the non-profit should be informed of just enough prospect research necessary to justify a solicitation level: last gift, highest gift, job title. Staff must be discreet. In that same vein, volunteers who are fundraising should never be given access to the donor database. Volunteers will respect the staff for respecting everyone's private data.

Commitments for Volunteers

Volunteers have different term commitments based on their skills for the most part. Individuals who volunteer to stuff envelopes and make phone calls may have open-ended commitments, and non-profits appreciate these kinds of volunteers who help out for years. When volunteers are invited to join advisory boards, they almost always ask how long their term of service is. A CEO who is asked to join a board of directors will tell the non-profit how much time they will devote to it. As a non-profit invites people to serve at higher levels, they will discover that their level of service has to match their availability. A member of the board of directors may be asked to serve a term of four years with the option to serve four more. As the board member reveals their talents and commitment, they may be asked to take on more responsibility: chair a committee, become an officer, participate in hiring high-level employees. Conversely, a problematic board member may not be invited to serve another term. The reasons to not ask a board member to re-up may include the member's interference in the day-to-day management of the organization.

Training Volunteers

Some non-profits schedule meetings with groups of volunteers on Saturdays in order to have time to generate enthusiasm, get the volunteers comfortable with the mission, explain the activity, and answer questions. They are called Super Saturday, Volunteer Day, Mission Day, and other names to pinpoint the focus. Some non-profits take volunteers through exercises to teach them important facts about the mission, how their work directly affects the people served by the non-profit, and the level of professionalism that is expected. Frequently, non-profits will have experts in their fields speak to the volunteers about critical aspects of the work so they are better informed. Frequently asked questions sheets can be distributed to give volunteers good responses in case they are asked about the mission. Fact sheets are also very helpful: the number of clients served, the amount of money raised, the improvement in clients' test scores, how many years the non-profit has been carrying out its mission, and how many employees and volunteers work for the non-profit.

Teaching Volunteers Solicitation Skills

Non-profits frequently deploy volunteers to solicit prospects and donors for annual gifts because peer-to-peer fundraising can be very effective. However, successful solicitation requires training and experience. It is the development director's duty to teach volunteers how to speak to prospects and donors about making gifts with nuanced phrases, listen to verbal clues, and notice body language. In the beginning, it's important to make volunteers successful so they will feel good about their accomplishments for the non-profit. Making them successful at fundraising can mean giving them very dependable donors to contact, with development directors knowing the donors will make their regular pledges. Some volunteers become very skilled at solicitation and they come to enjoy it for many reasons, so non-profits will deploy them several times to raise gifts. Others that are not as talented but, eager to help, can be asked to help with solicitations that are low risk; for example, they may ask them to solicit donors who are reliable for modest gifts or donors who are lapsed at modest giving levels.

Making the Best Use of Volunteers' Time and Talents

Making the best use of a volunteer's talent and the time they have available is a crucial task for the short term and long term. When non-profits engage people as volunteers, they are cultivating long-term donors, and those donors could be anybody. It's not uncommon for a very modest person serving as a volunteer to leave a large bequest to the non-profit. Often, people who cannot make major gifts from their cash flows or assets will write bequests into their wills. It's the most substantive way to make an impact on a mission. College professors have been known to leave large estate gifts to the colleges that employed them, librarians leave bequests to libraries, and doctors make provisions for their medical schools. But when a volunteer doesn't feel a strong affiliation to a past employer or college, they sometimes leave their estates to non-profits that they came to believe in through involvement. Making the best use of their time is to give them every opportunity to do what they want to do and what they're good at. Some volunteers like clerical tasks, others like planning events, and still others like to donate their professional skills as members of the board of directors. It's not appropriate to ask a retired CEO to lick envelopes, so development directors should outline some challenging work for retired professionals who are used to complex challenges.

Recruiting Volunteers

One of the confusing things a development director can tell a volunteer candidate is that they won't have to do too much work or commit to a large gift. Often development directors are so eager to get volunteers to sign up that they don't want to scare them off with an overwhelming agenda. Volunteers may wonder why they're being recruited at all if there will not be much to do. They tend to respect an institution and its leaders more when they are presented with challenging tasks. The conventional wisdom is to let volunteers decide what is too much. When development directors solicit volunteers for gifts, they sometimes ask for a specific amount and then equivocate. A better practice is to solicit for a specific amount and allow the individual to consider it and decide. Often an individual will give a lower amount if they have not yet volunteered and increase it with involvement. Volunteering and fundraising are all wrapped up together with the same objective.

Asking Professionals to Work for Non-profits at No Charge

Universities and colleges can often afford to pay attorneys' fees, but small non-profits commonly might not. A traditional practice has been asking attorneys to provide their services for free, and attorneys that value the exposure to wealthy board members may agree to volunteer. Often an attorney will volunteer to work on transactions when the non-profit buys or sells real estate. They may help out on employment and/or termination issues, including lawsuits that allege discrimination. When non-profits merge, they require quite a bit more time from an attorney. Sometimes non-profit boards will ask an attorney to write a document that puts into motion a compensation and benefit agreement for a CEO that plans to retire. When universities sell construction bonds in the bond market, an attorney and an investment banker will be required. Generally, universities don't disclose those compensation arrangements, if any. To further encourage attorneys to volunteer their time, non-profits appoint them to the board of directors where they are happy to meet potential new clients and to gain a reputation among board types for their expertise and service.

Asking Wealth Advisors and Investment Managers to Work at No Charge

Some non-profits have endowments that are managed by their own financial executives like treasurers. Non-profits that cannot afford to pay salaries for treasurers sometimes ask experienced wealth advisors or investment managers to join the board of directors to help them manage their endowments, improve the charity's financial management, examine wages, and find health insurance companies offering lower rates. Professional wealth managers can introduce new financial concepts, software, laws, and regulations to help a non-profit stay current in order to put it in the best financial position possible. They also can create financial scenarios to answer some pressing questions from other board members. For example, if another board member feels it's important to raise the hourly wages of the non-profit's workers, a financial expert can create a model of what a payroll with increased hourly rates would look like. They also can create a matrix to show the pros and cons of different health insurance companies' rates.

Orientation and Training for Volunteers

Volunteer orientation and training varies according to the level of expertise needed to do the job. Individuals who help out at social services agencies, for example, will require extensive training to understand and carry out their roles. This should be made clear at recruitment time and in orientation. Volunteers who call donors to renew their gifts also need extensive training and this also should be something explained at both orientation and training. One-on-one orientation and training is ideal, but for non-profits with small staffs, this is often impossible. A staff member will invite new volunteers to group meetings for orientation and to classes for training. Because people have different learning styles, staff can use visual aids, audio instruction, role playing, situational awareness, and video to help new volunteers learn about expectations. Using extensive amounts of time for orientation and training also will help staff weed out volunteers who don't fit their proposed roles. Prospective volunteers can use this time to reconsider their commitment and, if they don't feel they are a match, they can withdraw of their own volition. With time, volunteers end up serving in areas where they belong, and they become more skilled the longer they serve.

Motivating Volunteers

One of the best ways to motivate volunteers is to thank them profusely and often. Plus, acknowledgment and gratitude expressed by the top leadership is exceptionally meaningful and motivating. The fact that leaders who everyone respects says the volunteers are making a difference is very much appreciated, even though not all volunteers work to earn gratitude. However, most workers like praise whether they are paid or unpaid. One of the most effective ways to motivate volunteers is to have them meet the people they serve. For example, when they can meet children who have needs, the volunteers can get very involved in their lives. If they follow the children's progress as they get older, their work can go on for many years. On a different level, board members who get involved in the design and construction of new buildings may remain active while the buildings go up. Often, they are involved in their dedication.

Recognizing and Retaining Volunteers

Some volunteers enjoy attending annual luncheons or dinners where they receive awards and token gifts for their work. Non-profits that have space in their publications list the names of volunteers who have reached milestones in their years of accumulated service. When it's appropriate, non-profits feature a list of the names of volunteers in their publications. A very effective way to provide recognition is to feature a photo of a volunteer on the non-profit's website. This helps other friends of the non-profit see and appreciate the work these people do.

When the website shows a photo of the volunteer with a famous person, it increases the recognition factor even more. Some colleges and social services agencies feature photos of their volunteers working in other countries. If the work site is in the middle of a disaster zone or with a population under various threats, a photo of the volunteer in action is very powerful.

Evaluating Volunteers

One way to evaluate a volunteer is to offer them a questionnaire. It might ask the volunteer to read through a set of questions which ask them to rate things like how they enjoyed their experience, what they recommend to improve the experience, how it compared to other volunteer jobs they have had, how they value the mission, what they would suggest to improve the mission, who mentored them, and how effective they think they are with the people served. From their answers, development officers can pick up attitudes toward the mission, to administrators, and to the people who need the services. These attitudes can indicate if the volunteer's service should continue, be expanded or changed, or ended. Instead of the non-profit evaluating the volunteer, the volunteer evaluates themselves and the results tell management what should happen next. In a few cases, non-profits will evaluate a volunteer's performance because they are not representing the organization well. In these cases, development directors might work more intensely with a volunteer whose language or approach needs improvement. However, in the cases of volunteers who might do more harm than good, they may have to be released. In the case of a wealthy volunteer who is not performing well, the development director might direct the volunteer to a low-risk task. It can be worth the effort to redirect a wealthy volunteer for the benefits that involvement bring.

Role Board Members Play in Governing Non-profit

Members of a non-profit's board of directors write bylaws and set policies for many ways in which the organization will be managed. Typically, the board will direct the financial managers to follow the U.S. generally accepted accounting principles (GAAP) that are established by the Financial Accounting Standards Board, or FASB. The board will hold human resources managers accountable for following all federal and state employment laws specifically about sexual harassment, discrimination, wages, termination, and workers' compensation. Board members and staff are always concerned about violations of the law that may expose the non-profit to liability. Board members will approve fundraising goals for the organization and direct employees to follow the Donor Bill of Rights as it conducts solicitations and FASB accounting standards for reporting results. Typically, board members are prohibited from managing the daily operations of a non-profit unless they are invited to consult with management because of the board member's professional expertise.

Value of Diversity Among Non-profit's Volunteers

According to a study conducted by Blackbaud, volunteers who work for organizations that serve their interests will achieve better results. For example, alumni of a business school at a university may be very active in a group that provides welcomed networking opportunities. If alumni find new jobs through this kind of group, they will be more likely to volunteer to help. They will devote more volunteer time to make the alumni group successful and to make it even more effective. However, groups cannot function successfully without diversity. People with different backgrounds contribute knowledge that strengthens the organization. Diversity helps a non-profit grow because more people will be drawn in from many ethnic and racial groups, and non-profits must grow to survive. If organizations only appeal to donors in a narrow segment of the population, they will stagnate. If they stagnate, they will become stale and ultimately irrelevant. For example, if a Protestant denomination that is losing members is the only donor group that has traditionally supported a charity, the charity will ultimately fail. The charity must reach out and bring in volunteers from all interested groups.

Roles of Board Members in Governance and Management

Board members are responsible for hiring an attorney to write the non-profit's Articles of Incorporation, also known as a charter, and its bylaws. Both are required by the Internal Revenue Service when a non-profit applies for tax-exempt status. When its mission is modified or redirected because of external and internal factors, the board can change or rewrite its bylaws so the organization's work remains relevant. Board members have the fiduciary responsibility to steer the organization towards a sustainable future by adopting professional, sound, and ethical governance and financial management policies. Board members are responsible for ensuring that the non-profit has enough funding to sustain the mission. It sets policies for how the non-profit will be operated. Staff does not set policies and the board does not manage the day-to-day activities.

Roles of CEO in Governance and Management

The CEO, head of staff, is usually the Chairman of the board of directors. However, the CEO is responsible for managing the non-profit day to day and over the long term. The CEO supervises managers who run accounting, human resources, programs and services, maintenance, public relations, grant writers, facility directors, risk management, development, quality control, and transportation. The CEO seeks long-term outside funding like lines of credit and loans, represents the non-profit as it interacts with the state legislature, approves contracts with vendors, approves major accounts payable transactions, and acts as landlord if the non-profit owns the building. The CEO follows the policies set forth by the board, but they do not invite board members to co-manage the non-profit with them.

Responsibilities of Staff Members Who Govern and Manage Non-profits

Staff members are responsible for carrying out all of the policies set by the board of directors. Board members develop a strategic plan to give the staff direction, and the senior staff should avail itself of every opportunity to contribute to the plan. The staff is responsible for carrying out accounting, human resources, programs, quality assurance, fundraising, and marketing functions. Staff is directed to present updated reports to the board at least every quarter, but the comptroller may be required to report results to the board each month. A CEO and their senior staff may request an emergency meeting with the board chair when a crisis looms. While the CEO usually handles all legal matters, they may share the details of updates about lawsuits with the board. Most staff members do not participate in proceedings of the board when policies are established or revised, but staff may make recommendations to write new policies and amend existing policies when circumstances present opportunities to address operating challenges.

Trends and Preferences in Volunteering

Slacktivism

"Slacktivism" is a term coined in the last several years to refer to volunteers that want to help a non-profit for a short period of time without committing to long-range work. Slacktivists can jump into a fundraising drive for natural disasters like hurricanes, tornadoes, earthquakes, and tsunamis that destroy housing and infrastructure for millions of people. However, this kind of volunteer tends to be very busy working at a profession and has limited time to do anything outside of work. The numbers in this group are large and getting larger because volunteers today don't have the kind of time previous generations did.

Crowdsourcing

Non-profits have been using crowdsourcing for a very long time. A minister motivating a congregation to paint a women's shelter as a group, a corporation encouraging its employees to volunteer to work at a fun run, and the American Red Cross volunteers traveling to a disaster zone to help victims are all examples of crowdsourcing. The non-profit is pulling in all kinds of talents from a crowd to accomplish something large and significant.

Micro volunteering

Individuals with very short periods of free time can use their smartphones to be micro volunteers. Using their phones, they can sign petitions on Facebook or make an instant contribution to a cause, and they can do it with a click of their phones using apps that non-profits have distributed widely.

Structure of Non-profit Organization's Development Programs

A non-profit's structure will depend on its purpose, its scope, and what stage of development it is in. For example, a very small non-profit that is in its formation phase may begin with a small group of individuals who are dedicated to a mission: housing the homeless, building a school, or rescuing dogs and cats. The group may have the necessary skills to work with clients, and in the beginning, they may use their own funds or charitable gifts from their families. In the early days, a non-profit can see its effectiveness as it gets to know its clients. At some point, however, the non-profit realizes it should begin to find sustainable resources and it reaches out for help from people who have fundraising experience. It's common for non-profits to begin holding car washes and auctions because they require skills that many people have. As the non-profit grows, it looks for more ways to raise revenue to support salaries and programs. At this point, its board of directors will create gift acceptance policies and gift accounting procedures to meet FASB rules.

Functions of Non-profit Organizations

A non-profit is broadly described as an organization that functions to serve a societal need. It can be a need found in the general public or in broad areas like medicine, religion, education, hunger, animal welfare, immigration and many more. Within these broad areas it can focus on more narrow purposes such as finding a cure for Parkinson's Disease, saving the whales, providing scholarships to students, and sending food to Africa. Non-profits do not raise revenue to make profits; the organization does not distribute profits to its board and management. It invests all of its revenues back into the programs it produces to serve the public. In fact, because non-profits are not in existence to earn profits, they sometimes can run short of funds. The non-profit's board has fiduciary responsibility to keep the organization solvent. The program's employees are responsible for services to clients. The development office raises funds to fill holes in the budget and to fund expansion.

Culture of a Non-profit

A non-profit's culture varies widely. If a religious organization sponsors a non-profit, it will generally follow the constitution of the church's national organization. An education non-profit often follows the beliefs and attitudes of the founders, whether they're progressives or traditionalists. Anti-defamation groups can reflect the members' aggressive stand against prejudice. An animal welfare non-profit is often made up of people who work to save the lives of strays and promote rescues and adoption. Non-profits are not necessarily limited to one emotionally driven purpose, but their origins may have been in the observance of an egregious wrong that needed quick action to correct. As non-profits grow, their cultures may branch out into different subcultures that form around very specific interests. A children's agency may have its roots in religion, but as the agency changes with society's changing needs, its culture may become more clinical than religious. A non-profit that fights hunger may be domestically based and later evolve into a worldwide organization as it works in other countries.

Change in Culture and Structure of Non-profit over Time

Sometimes a non-profit's culture and structure have to change because of changes in the economy. For example, non-profits for the most part do not operate orphanages anymore because their operating costs are prohibitive. For that reason, most states will not pay non-profits to run them and they cannot afford to run them with private funds. Instead, children's non-profits place children into kindred placements, foster care, and adoptive homes with lower costs. Another example is the demise of women's Catholic colleges. Many decades ago, girls' Catholic high schools would be the

75

feeders to women's Catholic colleges where the curriculum was classic liberal arts. As the years moved forward, women began seeking colleges that also admitted men. They also sought out curriculums that offered education and training for specialized professions. In time, many of these colleges dissolved their associations with Catholic teaching orders and became secular higher education institutions. The ones that survived and thrived began to offer pre-law and pre-med courses, undergraduate and graduate degrees in business, and degrees in allied health profession majors like physical and occupational therapy. The challenge for development officers is to make effective cases for support of the non-profit's new missions when older donors only want to support their previous missions.

Leadership and Management

Mission Statements

A mission statement, crafted carefully, can tell a prospective donor exactly what the non-profit's mission is all about. Some non-profits can spend months drafting, editing, and rewriting their mission statements until everyone agrees it represents a true expression of their intent and results. They often begin with the word "to" or with a gerund verb such as "strengthening," "feeding," and "empowering." In general, they convey action that they take to fulfill needs, change lives, and improve conditions; and they are written with urgency and conviction. Mission statements alone are not enough to explain a non-profit's purpose in all of its complexity or challenges, however. Non-profits need other kinds of communications to promote the full picture of their work.

Vision Statements

Vision statements are different from mission statements. A vision statement is aspirational. It also is inspirational. It tells readers where the non-profit wants to go, and where it will go if everything goes right. It aspires to function at a higher level than it functions now. Its vision statement might be a departure from how they operated in the past. It could indicate that a non-profit is focusing on a few core key areas of work while it stops working in areas that are no longer relevant. A new vision statement might reflect changing conditions and how the non-profit is adapting to them in order to survive. When a non-profit crafts a new vision statement well, it should not imply that it is abandoning the mission of its founders.

Strategic Planning Methods

Conventional wisdom maintains that a board of trustees will have limited knowledge about how to create a strategic plan because (1) they've never created one before, (2) they don't know which best practices to use, (3) they don't ask for input from the staff, or (4) they don't understand that they have to invest in its success. A consultant can help the trustees begin creating the plan by demonstrating which practices are proven to achieve the best structure and results. Presentations by staff will reveal to the board many of the complexities of the non-profit that the trustees aren't aware of. Staff also can reveal what plans and actions have worked and what actions have failed and why. Rather than starting from scratch with very limited knowledge of facts, the board can ask the staff to bring them up to date on which issues from the past are no longer relevant and what today's challenges are. Instead of telling staff what actions to take, the board can involve staff thoroughly in the planning process to make it operate more efficiently.

Action Planning Methods in a Development Office

When a non-profit writes a strategic plan, it should concurrently write an action plan for each department. A development action plan starts with questions like, "What does the board want the development department to achieve?" Or, "How long does it have to deliver results?" The vice president of development can use the strategic plan to write goals for fundraising. For example, the goals might include how much the annual fund will increase over a period of five years. It could set a goal of raising a specific dollar amount in capital gifts for the capital campaign and describe how the process will accomplish its aim over how many years. Universities sometimes set participation goals: What percentage of alumni give now, and what do we want that number to be in five years? Staff assignments are made. The directors of the annual fund, planned giving, major gifts, and donor relations all will be given specific goals to be responsible for. The board can hear a presentation by the vice president of development who outlines the action plan. It can modify it—such as raising the goals, for example—or approve it.

Fundraising Program Evaluation Standards

One traditional method of evaluating fundraising is the cost per dollar raised (CPDR) metric. Non-profits simply can divide their fundraising expenses by their revenues. Many non-profits are very proud of their CPDRs and they quote this measure of success across many platforms. Participation rates can be important to universities. Each year, many universities try to raise their participation rates to demonstrate increasing support among alumni. Measuring donor retention is very important to all non-profits. It is easier to retain a donor than to acquire a new one, and also less expensive, so retention rates must be measured to track growth or lack thereof. Non-profits commonly report the average size of a charitable gift received, and as the average size grows, the organization should feel the difference. Conversion rates are often discussed. The definition would be how many new donors are converted from a pool of prospects.

Policy and Procedure Development

Policies are commonly established by the CEO and the board of trustees, while procedures are generally developed by the vice president of development. An example of a policy can be how the board wants to allocate bequests received from donors. The board could decide to deposit the entire amount of a bequest into the endowment to ensure its growth. Or it could write a policy that requires the non-profit to deposit 20 percent of every bequest into the endowment and the rest into general operating funds. A procedure means that the vice president would work with the comptroller to decide, for example, how to mechanically move the bequest from where it arrives electronically by wire transfer to the endowment. If the bequest is stock, the mechanisms for the stock to be received into the non-profit's account at a broker's office, to selling it, and depositing the funds into the non-profit's bank account are all details that become standard procedure for any non-profit. The same is true for major gifts.

Evaluating Policies and Procedures

Periodically, the board could take up their policy of how to put a bequest to use. If it deposits all of it into operating funds, how will the endowment grow? If it deposits all of it into the endowment, what impact does this have on the availability of operating funds? Should the policy be revised to require the bequest be split between the endowment and the operating fund? Should stock gifts from bequests be deposited into the endowment without selling it? Some boards have asked if the non-profit accepts gifts from companies that run gambling casinos. What is the moral effect of accepting gifts from casino and tobacco companies? Some boards have evaluated their endowments and divested themselves of stocks of companies they consider to be immoral. The vice president and the comptroller might evaluate their procedures with their stock brokerage and decide to change brokers. Or they may recommend that the non-profit change banks because they dislike the bank's procedures, to name another example.

Important Elements in Fundraising Plans

Annual Giving

Annual giving plans are generally based on the monetary goal that is set for the staff to achieve. Usually the goal is a percentage increase from the previous year's total dollars received. In order to achieve the goal, the leadership is advised to examine the annual budget; the current staff; which annual donors should be personally solicited for an annual gift and for what giving level; how many

78

donors should be solicited to reach the goal; how many prospects should be visited and who; how many active annual donors are in the database; how many previous donors might be expected to renew their gifts; how many mailings will be designed, printed, mailed, and when; how many telemarketing nights to schedule; what to create and change on the website to drive donors to the online gift page; what work to give to the active volunteer base; how to recruit more telemarketing callers; how to recruit students to form a senior class gift committee; which alumni to recruit to lead reunion gift committees; what premiums to offer; and how to measure the progress toward the goal at monthly intervals.

Planned Giving

It's difficult for planned giving to set an annual goal for fundraising because there is not a way to predict when a bequest will be received. Instead of focusing on annual goals, planned giving staff can take a long view of the cultivation of their constituency. Planned giving officers are most productive when they are spending time with planned giving donors and prospects. In the donor database, there is a code in a donor's file to indicate that they are a planned giving donor already or a prospect. There also is a code for which officers the prospects and donors are assigned to so there's no duplication. Travel and entertaining are large components of a planned giving budget and these expenses can be largely predicted based on past years. Some non-profits buy planned giving newsletters and brochures to send to their donors and prospects, and these annual expenses have to be factored in as well. Continuing education in planned giving is very important and officers can benefit from seminars and conferences where they can receive updates on estate planning laws and regulations. These costs also should be considered in the budget.

Major Gift

Major gift work stems from research on donors, prospects, and suspects. Planning the work begins with prospect research. Development directors can look at the research, qualify each prospect and donor, and create a list of priority people they will begin with. Then a strategy for each individual will be developed. Staff will be assigned to each prospect and donor so there is no overlap. Major gifts officers with extensive experience who will be hired will require higher salaries. Travel will be involved to visit major donors, and the budget will reflect travel costs. Non-profits and universities have traditionally been heavily dependent on special events to bring major donors and prospects closer to the people who manage the non-profit and to the people they serve. Doing special events for results requires event planners to contract with vendors, major gift officers to engage with attendees, the CEO or president to pay attention to the most important donors and prospects, and staff to inform the CEO of the major donors' backgrounds so they can inquire about their families and businesses.

Importance of Including Fundraising in Strategic Planning Process

A non-profit's strategic plan is commonly written to set goals that the board and management commit to completing successfully for a period in the future. For example, a strategic plan will routinely include goals to increase revenue, construct new facilities, expand programs, hire new staff, and develop new markets. A capital campaign is established to focus the work of fundraising within a specific time frame. The plan to increase revenue will include fundraising that requires the participation of the vice president of development. Working with the CEO, the development vice president will help guide the board toward realistic goals based on an analysis of the donor base and prospect pool. The board also can set goals for the types of funds that will be raised within the strategic plan. For example, the plan may call for an increase in restricted funds that could include scholarships, or an increase in the endowment that will produce investment income.

Impact of Organizational Structures on Effectiveness of Fundraising Programs

Organizational structures have significant impact on the effectiveness of every development program in every non-profit. The size of the non-profit may determine development goals and who will achieve them. In very small non-profits, the CEO may also be the fundraiser. Often, a CEO can be so bogged down in programmatic details that fundraising receives little attention. In such cases, the CEO may rely on a few fundraising techniques used in the past because they don't know any others: dinners with auctions and raffles, direct mail letters, and fun runs to name a few examples. However, when non-profits grow, they may hire development directors to lead fundraising full time. Plans to expand fundraising programs will require a larger budget, and that will impact the non-profit's cash flow. Sometimes when development departments become very large they will be spun off into a foundation whose money flows are separate from a non-profit, like a hospital. Hospital foundations collect charitable gifts and then award grants to doctors and researchers that work in the hospital. State universities also set up foundations to keep their donor records confidential. Public organizations like state universities must reveal their records to the public for inspection, but state university foundations are private and can protect their donors' confidential data.

Impact of Team Dynamics on Effectiveness of Fundraising Programs

Everyone in an institutional advancement office has to work together as a team in order for the fundraising program to be as effective as possible. Advancement employees can't work in silos. The alumni relations, event planning, and marketing staffs should always be recommending prospects they've met to the development officers. Development officers who meet potential donors at events can recommend the volunteer managers contact these potential donors to involve them to create some early cultivation. Employees who work in marketing and public relations at non-profits should accommodate development officers who want to have stories written and photos taken of donors they'd like to cultivate more. Development officers can feed to public relations some interesting leads about people connected to the non-profit even if they are not donor prospects. Employees outside the development office can be team oriented as well. The admissions office can feed the names of wealthy parents of current college students to the fundraisers.

Positive Effects of Working as a Team

Non-profits that have a national or global reach often create advisory boards to cultivate donors and potential donors in a way that lets them know they are very important to the mission. A national advisory board functions in similar ways to a board of trustees, the difference is that a national advisory board has no governing power or responsibilities. Typically, they meet quarterly at the non-profit's headquarters or on the university's campus. When these boards meet, the whole non-profit community can work for the common good and contribute to a day of presentations to keep the board members informed. The program staff can report on their work with people they serve and describe outcomes and challenges. An admissions staffer at a college can describe the results of recruitment and their projections. Finance heads can distribute current statements, explain the financial health of the non-profit, and explain areas of concern. Human resources managers can report on employee turnover and lawsuits against the non-profit. College deans can discuss new programs of study. All of these department representatives can make the advisory board members feel significant and needed—both great steps in the cultivation process.

Different Kinds of Development Professionals Working as a Team

Development officers that work in planned giving, annual giving, major gifts, principal gifts, reunion giving, cold calling, and appointment setting can all work together as a team by keeping the needs of each specialty in mind. When they work together, they can achieve the departmental goals that have been set and the individual goals they have written for themselves. Planned giving officers should be invited to attend events planned for annual fund donors so they can meet and identify potential planned giving prospects. Principal gifts officers should be invited to attend planned giving social events for the same purposes. Annual giving officers should be invited to reunion gift meetings and events to identify and qualify prospects for annual giving leadership roles. Major gift officers should be invited to attend regional meetings and events so they can meet people who are not normally on their donor or prospect lists. The purpose of this kind of teamwork and inclusion is for development officers in several different areas to meet new prospects in person so that when they want to contact them by phone or email, there is already a frame of reference. It reduces the chance of a development officer giving the impression that they are making a cold call or random call. The development officer has met the prospect, references the event to refresh the prospect's memory, and invites the prospect to a new event or to just a casual conversation over coffee to assess their interest in involvement. The prospect not only makes a decision based on the phone call, but also on their impression the development officer has made at the event.

Ensuring Integrity of Development Office's Database

It's common for a database to have many incorrect donor addresses because people move all the time and don't notify every organization that mails to them. The best way to update donor addresses is to run the database through the U.S. Post Office's National Change of Address software (NCOA). The USPS maintains address changes for hundreds of millions of Americans. The best practice is to run the database through NCOA once per year. This step will save money in the direct mail program. Another way to ensure the integrity of the database is to limit the number of employees that can enter and change data. Often, the director of advancement services is the only staff member that can enter or change data. This can prevent duplication of records, which is a universal problem with non-profit databases. Some trusted major gift and planned giving officers can be granted permission to enter and change data after they have made a donor call and they have discovered important changes.

Securing Donor Data Against Hackers

There are many reasons to worry about the security of a donor database. Malware and viruses could interfere with the operation of the database. Hackers can use the non-profit's web interface to break into the system and steal very important donor data, including donors' credit card numbers, gift ledgers, addresses, phone numbers, and email addresses. Non-profits that don't limit access to the donor database risk theft of important data by employees who should not be in the system. For non-profits that accept credit cards or debit cards for charitable gifts, they must be in compliance with the Payment Card Industry Data Security Standards. For the most part, the manufacturer of the donor software should guarantee the non-profit that the software has safeguards to protect the data. This is very important for small non-profits that don't have an information technology staff with enough sophistication to prevent firewall breaches in the donor database.

Development Audits

A development audit is a thorough examination of all of the functions of the development office: the annual fund programs, major gifts, planned giving, donor database management, gift accounting, alumni relations, public relations, grant writing, special event planning, gift acknowledgement, budget, continuing professional development, support, and job descriptions for all of the employees.

<u>Components</u>

For example, development consultant who performs the audit may ask these questions:

- How well are the functions staffed?
- How experienced are the supervisors?
- Are the employees being trained to do their jobs and how?
- What are the fundraising goals and are they meeting them?
- Does the department follow its own budget?
- Does it need more funding?
- Is the department following established policies and guidelines?
- Is it following the strategic plan?
- Does it spend productively and efficiently on special events?
- What does it charge attendees for special events, and should they charge more?
- Is the CEO involved in fundraising?
- Is the board of directors involved in fundraising?
- Who opens gift envelopes and what's the procedure for depositing gifts?
- How are gifts acknowledged and how fast?
- Who is authorized to access the donor database?
- What version is the database software?
- What's the average gift?
- Who decides if a gift is unrestricted or restricted?
- How well attended are events?
- Have donors been surveyed about their opinions of the non-profit? What are the results?

Budgeting Process

There is considerable controversy in some non-profits about not looking at fundraising as overhead because of the negative connotations the term "overhead" carries. Sometimes non-profits are strongly encouraged to reduce their overhead so that the ratios look better to major funders. Non-profits that reduce their fundraising budgets because they consider fundraising "overhead" are buying into what Stanford University economists call the starvation cycle. The more they reduce fundraising to reduce costs, the more they risk the health and future of the non-profit as they run out of money. It is a very high-risk move and not feasible over the long term. When non-profits create their annual budget, the most senior development director should be part of the process. They should project how much the department will raise and how much it will cost to meet their goal. Non-profits that skimp on development staff, direct mail, events, and online giving are very much at risk of becoming financially unstable.

Reporting Financial Statements

Non-profits report their statement of financial position, statement of activities, cash flow from operating activity, and program services. Non-profits report their financial results on IRS form 990, which many of them link to online from their websites. 990s are relatively easy to read. They are also available on the Foundation Center's website and GuideStar's website. Interested parties can examine the form to find annual revenue from contributions, program service revenue, investment income, and revenue from grants and events; total salaries and other compensation for the staff, professional fundraising fees, and other expenses; total assets, total liabilities, the compensation of the highest-paid executives, and the value of endowment funds. The form also will show the value of securities sold, if they were sold at a profit or a loss, and the dollar amount increase or decrease in the total value of the endowment. Most non-profits also include a long statement of their missions, their religious motivations (if any), their clients' needs and how they were served, the scope of their work (geographic, in most cases), and a brief statement of their history.

Non-profit Audit

An audit of a non-profit is not required by the IRS or by the federal government, except in cases where non-profits are receiving substantial revenue from the federal government in terms of grants. A non-profit can hire an auditing firm or a CPA to do an annual audit if it is required by the board of directors or requested by the CEO. Typically, an audit report will make minor suggestions on how a non-profit might adjust its processes. More often than not, it will be made available to anyone who requests it in order to be totally transparent to the public. For example, when applying to a major foundation for a grant, a non-profit may be required to send a copy of their audit report with the application to the foundation staff. Similarly, foundations and governments may require a copy of an audit to be filed with them annually as part of the stewardship/reporting process. If a non-profit is very small, however, it may not make sense to pay a large fee for auditing services.

Market Research

Market research can tell non-profits many things about their fundraising, including what it does right and what it can improve. By asking donors to take a survey, market research experts can determine things like what is the non-profit's core fundraising audience, how has it changed over the years, what has the non-profit done to keep current with the changes, what keywords and graphics inspire donors to give, what words and graphics discourage donors, how many segments of donors there are and if the non-profit is targeting its message to all of them, what event or events are stopping donors from renewing their gifts, is the mission still relevant, how easy is the mission to understand, how easy it is to make a gift to the non-profit, what factors have drawn donors to other non-profits, if donors didn't renew because they're making gifts to help agencies that respond to disasters, and how likely are they to come back once the disaster is over.

Integrated Marketing

Non-profits have increasingly moved to an integrated marketing model to send consistent messages to all of the non-profit's diverse constituents. For example, a university may use integrated marketing to make sure their admissions and development departments are sending consistent messages with their graphics and words to create the same image. Other non-profits use integrated marketing to make their messages consistent over Twitter, Facebook, YouTube, their websites, printed materials, presentations, public relations, signage in public places, and videos so that they send one important message all of the time. Without integrated marketing, constituents can become misinformed, confused, or disinterested because they can't figure out what the non-profit is all about. This is particularly important when a non-profit's mission has evolved, and the CEO does not want its image to get stuck in past work that the non-profit doesn't do any more.

Measuring Impact on the Community

When non-profits apply for grants, they are often asked how they will measure their effectiveness in the community if they become recipients. It's a complex question but answering it will result from a lengthy and detailed process of how to set up the metrics for such a process. In social services agencies, it may not be easy to show results in the short term because family issues can take a great deal of time to resolve with therapy and education before they take a positive turn. Common measurements of impact, for example, include surveying clients for their opinions about a non-profit's effect on their lives, measuring an increase or decrease in incidents the non-profit works to prevent, charting changes in physical and mental health resulting from the non-profit's treatment offerings, tracking graduation rates, and others. It's important for the grantor and the recipient to agree on how results should be measured and then to share each other's evaluations of the results.

Resources Used in Training Officers

Planned Giving Officers

Planned giving is considered both an art and a science. Planned giving directors must have the personality to establish and maintain relationships with older people. They must have mathematical skills as well to calculate accurately charitable gift annuities, trusts, tax implications, and to understand state laws that regulate these vehicles and comply. There are several good planned giving training programs taught all year by attorneys who also are available over the long term to answer questions. However, mentoring is the best way to teach new planned giving officers. Teaching by example is very effective, especially when new staff can join experienced directors on calls with donors. Planned giving is not something that can be learned quickly, even for lawyers that join development departments. In the long run, a combination of people skills and improved legal and financial knowledge will make a planned giving officer more effective.

Annual Giving Officers

Unlike planned giving, annual giving training can be focused on learning mechanical functions. Most non-profits have direct mail guidelines that recommend the language style, topics, graphics, copy length, and the amount of detail used in their direct mail letters. They may vary their envelopes to encourage donors to open them, and they may code envelopes to track which direct mail packages worked the best. The non-profit's donor database may have standard programs that will pull mailing lists to match each letter and envelope. If not, programs can be written to extract the data. Non-profits have policies about postage, frequency, and donors to be solicited. New annual fund directors can learn all of it with practice. They also can learn telemarketing. If the non-profit used volunteers or paid callers, they must be recruited, trained, scheduled, and monitored, all of which can be learned. Non-profits will have policies and procedures about callers' scripts, wages, how aggressive they should be, and when they should be retained or dismissed. New staff also can be trained to assemble all of the callers' paperwork and send out pledges the next day to the donors reached. Inserts can be printed prior to telemarketing seasons, including response envelopes, tips on giving through the website, short explanations of corporate matching gifts, and friendly reminders about bequests and annuities. Development offices may institute a policy that telemarketing pledge reminders be mailed first class instead of bulk.

Major Gift Officers

Major gift officers often begin their careers as annual fund officers, and they are trained in this capacity to solicit annual fund gifts. They develop their solicitation skills by asking donors for one-year pledges first, and then by asking for multi-year pledges. Development officers who cultivate their donors effectively can ask them to increase their giving step by step and, after several years, donors' giving may increase dramatically. Major gift officers work in the same way, cultivating donors over a period of several years and planning solicitations. The difference is that major gift officers are relieved of programmatic duties like planning events, writing and producing direct mail, hiring callers and running telemarketing, organizing reunion gift campaigns, sending out premiums, and running giving club events. They are focused on traveling to spend time with donors all over the country. So while there is no special major gift officer training, mentors who are senior major gift officers can effectively teach by example.

Board Members

The first step in training board members is convincing them they need training. Some board members who have long tenures will say they have a lot of experience and don't need training. A consultant has recommended giving board members a fundraising quiz for them to evaluate themselves as effective cultivators and solicitors. If they admit they could use more training, there are different ways to begin the process. Sometimes board members seek out consultants and seminar speakers to learn some development fundamentals. They hire consultants to work with board members on learning cultivation and solicitations skills, attend development seminars and conferences, and read books on fundraising. Often it is effective for a current member of the board to introduce fundraising training with their peers. If this board member is highly respected and esteemed by other board members, this person can be a highly credible trainer that everyone will listen to. This board member can go beyond training and use different techniques to inspire and motivate their colleagues to begin their development work.

Human Resource Management Principles Within Institutional Advancement Departments

The subject of searching for and hiring development professionals is first on the list of many ways in which a human resources department provides services to a development staff. An experienced human resources manager will seek to understand what a development job is really all about—its depth, scope, level of sophistication, and very specialized skills and experience. Development is both an art and a science, and it is very important for a human resources manager to work with the hiring manager to agree on what qualities they seek in new hires. The hiring manager should write the job description for everyone they hire, and human resources will assist. Human resources specialists can screen out inappropriate resumes, take calls inquiring about the job, make calls to applicants to set up interviews, and check references. Many non-profits require background screening that human resources can arrange in addition to physicals, TB tests, and drug screening.

Assistance from Human Resources Department

Human resources can assist a development office in leadership practices. Setting up a review process and schedule can help development managers schedule regular performance reviews with staff as a motivation tool. Employees who receive regular feedback about their work feel appreciated and valued, and they find it to be a motivator. Managers who are assisting some employees can help them improve their performance with regular reviews. In that same vein, managers that document their problems with workers receive more support from human resources if they have to terminate the workers. Human resources can create the concept of mentoring in a development department by teaching supervisors and employees what mentoring is and encouraging employees to find and connect with mentors. Succession plans are also important programs that human resources can create to be ready when a senior vice president or a CEO is going to retire.

Human Resources Strategies Applied to a Development Department

Human resources can help the development staff plan strategies for hiring fundraising specialists for programs including upcoming capital campaigns, a new series of events designed for cultivation, a new planned giving program, and for hiring managers with extensive development experience. A human resources manager can prepare a presentation to a non-profit's board of directors in which they explain the need for new staff to play new specialized roles to carry out new programs. They can work with the board and the development vice president to write job descriptions everyone can agree on. As this process develops, the board and current staff can recommend development professionals with great reputations. Often, staff-recommended candidates make some of the best hires. A human resources manager may say, as they often do, that the best predictor of future performance is the record of past performance.

Approaches to Job Design in a Development Office

Engineering Approaches

In a development office, managers commonly use the engineering method of designing jobs. They begin with the amount of money they want to raise through annual giving, major gifts, and planned gifts. They want to raise more money in every category of giving than was raised the year before. From these dollar goals, they write job descriptions to outline precisely what each development officer must do to raise the money and then they ask the officers every month to describe their activities in great detail to show how well they are following their job descriptions. This engineering approach can work well with annual fund directors and their staffs because these kinds of gifts come in quickly and the goal will be reached by using formulas that have proven to work. However, major gifts and planned gifts don't come in on a schedule to help development managers meet their goals. Major gifts take time—sometimes years—to come to fruition, and they are given on the donor's timetable, not the institution's. The same can be said for planned giving gifts. Bequests are received when donors die, and those dates are not something that can be planned. Even if a planned giving director is selling charitable gift annuities, there is not necessarily a timetable that donors will follow. They will make their decisions and send in their contracts independently.

Personal Approaches

Instead of writing precisely worded job descriptions and forcing development officers to adhere to a prescribed set of activities that they report every month, some development managers take a personal approach and focus on what each staff member does best and allows them to do it. For example, a development officer who is very technically oriented—maintains a database in an efficient and excellent way—probably is not someone who should spend time in donor-facing situations. This kind of personality should be encouraged to find ways to improve development services because they enjoy it and excel in it. Similarly, a development officer who is outgoing with familiar donors and strangers alike should be encouraged to go to more events and meet more people who might do the organization a lot of good. Encouraging both kinds of personalities to pursue activities they perform well will also promote learning and growing because they will find new challenges.

Rewards Approach

A job and tasks within the job have to be personally rewarding to most employees; in fact, most employees of a non-profit seek employment there because they anticipate they will do rewarding work. When a non-profit employee accomplishes a great task and it improves the lives of others, that employee ought to feel personally and professionally rewarded. If a development officer is permitted to use all of their skills and talents to accomplish a task, the task will take on an enormous sense of importance to them personally and its completion will be their reward. Development work is difficult, so praise from a development director and a CEO goes a long way toward making a development officer feel appreciated and thanked. That kind of appreciation is a major motivating factor for the employee to do their next task with confidence: that someone in management is paying attention and they will be praised and thanked when they succeed at their next effort.

Professional Roles in a Fundraising Department

Annual Fund Director

The annual fund director is chiefly responsible for consistent gift revenue flowing into the non-profit. Direct mail and telemarketing tend to be seasonal, but gifts should be cultivated and solicited all year. The annual fund director will spend time with donors and prospects on a regular basis to solicit annual gifts in the $1,000 to $5,000 range. They will direct the design, production and mailing of direct mail solicitation packages on a schedule that database research shows is the most productive. The same is true for the telemarketing schedule. The annual fund director at a university also will assign the senior class gift and reunion gifts to associates. Travel to visit and solicit annual gifts also is in the annual fund director's purview, and travel must be scheduled around important special events. The annual fund director also will supervise the volunteer donor committee assigned to solicit annual fund gifts in the $1,000 range and up.

Planned Giving Director

The planned giving director is responsible for managing a sophisticated group of employees that has a very good blend of people skills and technical knowledge in estate planning. The director of planned giving will assign prospects to planned giving officers who will qualify them, make contact, visit, create relationships, and devise long-range strategies that are designed to bring in the largest gifts any non-profit will ever receive. The planned giving director will purchase the software necessary to calculate charitable gift annuities in house, and they will create professional relationships with attorneys who might be consulted on matters of estate planning. Cooperating with other development functions is crucial because annual fund, major gifts, and planned giving directors are in competition for many of the same prospects. A successful development office will set policies and procedures for donor assignments, temporary clearances, coordinated solicitations, and specific cultivation coordination to encourage different directors to work together for what is best for the non-profit.

Major Gifts Director

The major gifts director has the responsibility of raising larger gifts than those typically at the annual fund level, and gifts that are given in a more outright way than planned gifts. Major gift officers don't necessarily have to possess the same estate planning knowledge that planned giving officers have. Their goal is to move donors to a decision on making major gifts in a shorter time frame. As in annual fund work, major gift directors create a sense of urgency with donors. They may discuss that it's urgent to make a gift soon to begin construction of a building or to get endowed scholarships in place to begin earning funds to alleviate student tuition burdens. Major gifts directors travel frequently to visit and spend time with donors to learn their interests, involve them in non-profit activities that interest them, and coordinate visits to the non-profit.

Culture of Philanthropy

A culture of philanthropy means everyone in the non-profit is aware of the importance of philanthropy and everyone participates in it. True development work is not just about transactions with donors. It's about emphasizing how important it is for everyone in the non-profit being aware of every contact and impression they make with donors, and to consider how their behavior might help further good relationships with them. From the receptionist who answers a donor's call to the program directors who run the non-profit's mission, everyone is aware of being "donor centric." Development directors need program directors to help provide content for thank-you letters to donors, and for presentations which will include stories about the kinds of real needs the non-profit is fulfilling. Finance managers are needed to cooperate with grant writers who are preparing detailed proposals to send to foundations and corporations. Social workers are needed to cooperate in getting people who have received help to speak at dinners to show donors' appreciation. Board members are responsible not just for governance but for bringing in new donors and helping solicit existing donors for larger gifts.

Tools to Assess Needs for Contracted Services

A needs assessment survey can be conducted with employees to gather opinions about what are the group's most pressing needs. While there is obvious agreement that some functions that are necessary cannot be handled in house, the specific needs for outside contractors can rise to the top. Another tool is benchmarking. If an organization can compare its revenues and expenses to other similar non-profits by using the same metrics, it may reflect a need for contracted services in the revenue-producing area or in the support areas including accounting, database maintenance, human resources, and public relations. A risk assessment can be done to weigh the choices of using contracted service companies vs. doing the work in house or doing nothing at all, which also is a choice. An examination of the organization's budget can determine if there are funds to pay for an assessment and if there are funds to pay for contracted services.

Hiring Fundraising Consultants for Capital Campaigns

Non-profits that seek a professional consultant for a capital campaign would begin by thoroughly discussing internally the need to raise capital gifts. First, the board of directors and the CEO should be in complete agreement that the non-profit needs a capital campaign to build additional facilities to expand program offerings. A capital campaign committee of the board would be formed. An architect can be hired to design basic drawings of new buildings and provide a cost estimate for the entire project. With this estimate in hand, the committee and the CEO may proceed with a presentation to the full board. After discussions and approval, the committee may take on the task of developing a complete campaign budget. Within this budget are fees the board would pay a capital campaign consultant to help guide the process. Once the non-profit knows how much it can afford to pay a consultant, it will distribute a request for proposal (RFP) in media that are read widely by consultants. The committee also may send the RFP to consultants it has worked with before. When reviewing the proposals, the committee will consider each consultant's history of helping campaigns succeed, their price quote, their careers in fundraising before they became consultants, and references from clients. All of this information will help the non-profit make its choice.

Managing Consultants for Capital Campaigns

A non-profit that hires a campaign consultant will tell the consultant what their role or roles will be. The consultant may be hired to analyze the board's strengths to determine if it is ready for a capital campaign. How much are board members currently giving, and what is their potential for giving capital gifts during a campaign? How influential can they be in soliciting gifts from friends and acquaintances for a capital campaign? Should any board members be replaced? What kind of board members should be brought on board for the campaign? The consultant may be assigned to evaluate staff for an upcoming campaign. What is their fundraising record? What donors are they assigned to? What training do they need to be effective during a campaign? A consultant may be assigned to find new and outside donors for a campaign. They may be asked to connect the CEO to influential people in the community to recruit new board members. Above all, the development consultant should be given an agenda and told specifically what their assignments are.

Evaluating Campaign Consultants or Development Consultants

A CEO or a development vice president may evaluate a consultant by comparing their results to their assignments. If a consultant is tasked with raising money, how much have they raised and how much were they assigned to raise? Or, if a consultant was assigned to work with the board to make their own capital gifts and raise gifts from others, the consultant can be evaluated on expectations vs. results. A consultant might be hired to help development officers learn new skills and their effectiveness can be assessed based on the staff members' activity. Some non-profits hire consultants to help improve their fundraising web page content and mechanisms to make gifts easily. They might be tasked with designing and writing new capital campaign brochures and other collateral that explains the campaign's goals and provides architectural renderings of new buildings on the drawing board. Event planning to accomplish strategic goals also is something a consultant can assist with or carry out completely.

Evaluating and Selecting Telemarketing Vendors

When non-profits are too small to hire a staff member to recruit, train, and put paid telemarketers to work, they frequently contract with a non-profit fundraising firm. The outside firm hires its own callers and trains them on the mission of the non-profit, including why it needs charitable contributions. The firm asks the non-profit for data on its donors, and the non-profit transmits the data which includes names, addresses, the amount of the last gift, and employer matching gift information. Non-profits have to carefully calculate the costs of such services and weigh the cost against the total dollar amount that is pledged. The development manager also must ask how are the callers trained, how well do they explain the mission, and how well are they writing down questions that the development staff can follow up with. Are the best callers paid bonuses for bringing in large gifts by phone? Do they receive increases in their hourly wages when they raise their productivity? What questions do the callers have for the non-profit?

Evaluating Direct Mail Vendors

Most non-profits have come to the conclusion that they cannot handle all of the processes of direct mail in house if they want to be effective. The process includes designing the package, writing a letter from the CEO, writing testimonials, taking high-quality photos, and calculating the expenses involved in a direct mail campaign like the cost to print the package and postage. Most direct mail companies will handle everything, including processing data from the non-profit's database. Before deciding on a vendor, non-profits can determine their goals: how many gifts are desired from one mailing, how many increased gifts are expected, and how many new gifts are predicted. After the vendor puts the package together and mails it, its effectiveness can be measured fairly quickly. Responses will be received within weeks, after which they will taper off. If the results are average, the non-profit could do market research to learn how the direct mail package could be improved. If the same vendor returns average results, non-profits should evaluate the whole process to learn what must change.

Selecting, Managing, and Evaluating Attorney Advisors

Some large non-profits that have large endowments, take on high-risk programming, or provide healthcare often have general counsels and working relationships with outside law firms to handle litigation. Non-profits look for law firms that have experience defending universities, medical centers, social services agencies, animal rights non-profits, and others from individuals who have sued. They handle the mergers of non-profits, and they can become involved in regulatory compliance tasks. Employment law and employee benefits are key areas as well. Health insurance

and workers' compensation issues are often under an attorney's purview. Any contracts a non-profit enters into with a vendor would be reviewed by an attorney. Planned giving agreements and contracts do not always have to be reviewed by outside attorneys, but it is still a good practice, especially when in doubt. A non-profit can evaluate an attorney who is considered to be a candidate in different ways: they ask about how an attorney might handle a given scenario, to describe important cases they handled in the past, work with them on a project for their bar association and seek referrals from other general counsels of other non-profits.

Evaluating Providers of Donor Databases

Non-profits seek specific database software to record charitable gifts from donors and to produce reports of donation activity. A non-profit may ask a provider to present facts about its capacity to save data, secure the data, and to write automated reports that virtually all non-profits require. These records begin with a gift ledger for each donor and, using this ledger, reports will specify the years during which they were donors and the amount donated each year, the club levels assigned to donors based on their annual gifts, whether or not the gift was matched, the type of gift that was donated, and the total amount given during a donor's history. Non-profits also may ask a provider to support multiple ratings for each donor, the names of employers and the donor's job title, the names of family members, the development officer assigned to the donor, and space for lengthy notes about donors after visits or during ongoing prospect research. Using all of this data, a non-profit will seek a database provider that can accept coding instructions from a development officer to produce non-automated reports that analyze the data.

Managing Meetings

Current advice from business leaders on running the best meetings:

- The meeting convener should decide what they want to accomplish in the meeting.
- Set a time limit for the meeting and stick to it.
- Assign an employee to take minutes and then distribute the minutes afterward.
- Write an agenda and place priority discussion items first.
- Distribute the agenda to everyone before the meeting so attendees have time to prepare.
- Invite people to attend only for the length of time their participation requires.
- Use a meeting location that minimizes noise and instruct the staff to not interrupt.
- Make sure all participants know why each other is attending.
- Use the best technology for presentations and learn how to use it.
- Keep meetings small so participants feel safer about speaking openly.
- Schedule breaks frequently.
- Plan for "parking lot time" after the meeting so the attendees can continue talking casually and share recommendations, solutions, research, and contacts.

Managing Change in an Organization

According to a study by the consulting firm McKinsey and Co., managing change within an organization requires four conditions to be successful: (1) a purpose to believe in, (2) reinforcement systems, (3) the skills required for change, and (4) consistent role models. If employees believe in the organization's purpose, they will adapt more easily to change. New, consistent behavior by senior management convinces staff that the change is real and that everyone at the top buys into it. Large-scale change happens slowly. Management can't teach everything there is to know about how change will happen in one meeting. Rather, supervisors could teach in small time periods, with time in between for the staff to work with the new principles. Everyone in management

90

must change their behavior, not just the senior members. Line supervisors also must change for all employees to believe it.

Effective Leadership in Development Offices

In a standard development office, the leadership is usually a vice president of the non-profit. The vice president hires a staff to carry out development programs and managing them well can make the operation successful. Managing well is a complex job, and there are some important principles the vice president can follow: (1) Treat staff like individuals, not like functions. A vice president that models this behavior will motivate everyone who feels appreciated and necessary. (2) Treat all staff from all over the organization with respect and it will raise their cooperation level and desire to help when needed. (3) Remove the things that stop staff from doing their jobs to their fullest. (4) Empower staff with resources and permission to do their best. (5) Model ethical and professional behavior and set the standard for others. Individuals inside and outside the non-profit will notice it and respect it. (6) Advocate for the staff with top management. (7) Show that some mistakes aren't fatal. (8) Don't assign a task to staff that management would not do.

Mentoring Roles and Functions Essential for Effective Management

A senior development manager owes their staff regular ongoing mentoring in order for the whole development function to be effective. Many employees in a typical development office are young and full of enthusiasm and mentoring them enables them to acquire skills and seasoning. Senior managers have experienced successes and failures, and often they can guide young employees away from practices that are ineffective or that can lead to problems. They also can recommend tactics that are proven and suggest them to young employees who are eager to learn. Opening up a teaching or mentoring dialogue makes it easier for employees to seek out advice and ask questions. Mentors can teach their mentees about office politics and board politics and help them avoid unproductive situations and be effective in others' eyes. In addition, mentors have the responsibility of explaining what legal and ethical practices must be followed and why. The more a mentor emphasizes legal and ethical practices, the more the staff will understand how high the mentor's standards are and they will work to meet them.

Principals of Leadership

The person in a leadership position must be dependable and consistent. Staff must be able to count on management to be present to make decisions that are fair, firm, and that follow policies that everyone is familiar with. Managers must exercise good judgment when situations arise that have no reference in policies and no historical precedence. Sometimes these judgments are called imperfect because they must be made quickly, and a perfect decision may never be possible. Management must be counted on to be assertive to accomplish what the department or the entire organization needs even if the task is difficult and/or unpleasant. Leaders are hired and paid well to use their experience taking on duties that many others on staff may not want to do or would not do. While they are being assertive, management also must be seen as having integrity, which is defined as a person that never wavers from their moral code. Leaders with integrity are respected as individuals who are always true to their own high standards and who don't abandon their character when a difficult situation arises. Effective leaders also are resilient, and they don't expect their staff to endure more than they do. They don't force a staff member to confront a difficult situation because they can't, and they don't leave an event early because they are tired so staff has to rearrange furniture and clean up on their own.

Sources of Information About Philanthropy

Historical Sources

The National Philanthropic Trust, the Open Philanthropy Project, Learning to Give, Philanthropy Round Table, Charity Navigator, and the Johnson Center for Philanthropy are productive sources for information about the history of philanthropy in the Unites States.

Contemporary Sources

GuideStar, the Foundation Center, Chronicle of Philanthropy, the National Philanthropic Trust, the Foundation Source, Charity Watch, GrantSpace, Charity Navigator, Giving USA, Forbes, Fortune, and the Blackbaud Institute are all excellent sources for information about contemporary philanthropy in the United States.

Books on Fundraising

The following are some writers of books on fundraising and the titles of those books that are available to development professionals:

- Jerold Panas, author of Asking
- Kay Sprinkel Grace, Fundraising Mistakes That Bedevil All Boards
- Marc Pitman, Ask Without Fear
- Penelope Burk, Donor-Centered Leadership
- Joe Garecht, How to Raise Money for Any Non-profit
- Andrea Kihlstedt and Andy Robinson, Train Your Board (and Everyone Else) to Raise Money
- Amy Eisenstein, Major Gift Fundraising for Small Shops
- Richard Perry and Jeff Schreifels, It's Not Just About the Money
- Adrian Sargeant and Jen Shang, Fundraising Principles and Practice
- Tom Ahern, How to Write Fundraising Materials That Raise More Money
- Roger Craver, Retention Fundraising

Organizational Development

A non-profit uses organizational development when it has a problem and the non-profit senses that it needs to change something. Sometimes the problem is a staff member who is not performing, not getting along with their supervisor or work group, or does not know how to do their job. Or the problem could be something else. The non-profit sets organizational development in motion to fully assess the situation, either by an outside consultant or by someone internal. The assessment can be conducted through interviewing the staff, by interviewing other staff members that interact with it, and by having staff fill out questionnaires or surveys. Once the information is collected, an analysis can reveal the problem. When there is agreement about the source of the problem, then the non-profit can plan how it will intervene to solve it. Sometimes an intervention means that someone or more than one person on the staff needs training to do their jobs. Sometimes a process or program is obsolete and needs to be changed. Other interventions might include training the leadership on better management practices. Sometimes staff are terminated to fix the problem. After the intervention, the process should be evaluated.

Organizational Climate

Organization climate refers to the prevailing attitudes present in the majority of employees of a corporation or a non-profit. An outside consultant can review an organization and find, for example, that the majority of its employees are unhappy about their low wages. A climate review might reveal that some employees don't like the CEO and they have spread rumors about him or her to turn more employees negative. It also could uncover a prevailing attitude that more than half of the employees are being asked to do tasks they don't know how to do, or the organization requires them to work too many hours to complete tasks that should take less time. It might help management understand that their decisions are not always derived from wisdom that could have been learned easily from talking with front-line staff or donor-facing development officers. Organizational climates also can turn negative or fearful when a merger with another organization is on the horizon; employees are worried about losing their jobs or having to work under a different structure they have already decided they don't like.

Interventions to Put Organizational Structure on the Path to Higher Productivity

There are several ways to intervene in an organization that needs to change. The employees can go through educational programs that will teach them about what management wants to accomplish and how it wants staff to help getting there. They can be taught the importance of goal setting and are asked to set their own goals so they buy into the process. Staff can be asked to discuss the outside threats against the organization and what they can do to protect it. It also can identify opportunities to increase donor contributions, save expenses, motivate staff, and increase trust. An outside interventionist can examine a team and evaluate its effectiveness; changes to the team can be made to increase its chances of being successful. Management can identify employees that are not on board with the organization's goals and have demonstrated they will never be—either for unknown or personal reasons—and terminate them.

Ethics, Accountability, and Professionalism

Federal Regulations That Affect the Operation of Non-profit Organizations

The Internal Revenue Service (IRS) has promulgated detailed regulations for non-profits that all development directors should at least be aware of and preferably be intimately familiar with. The most important is that, in order to be exempt from paying taxes, a non-profit should apply for and receive a 501(c)(3) designation from the IRS. Individuals may not be aware that this is necessary, but foundations and corporations are. In fact, when applying for grants, most organizations will state this requirement up front in their lists of criteria. Non-profits also are required by the IRS to complete and file form 990 that lists their finances in detail. The form lists, among many other things, how much money is spent on administrative salaries, events, lobbying, and fundraising activities by outside firms. The 990 also shows any potential conflicts of interest if a relative of a board member is hired for a fee. 990s of foundations are frequently examined in detail by prospect researchers who are interested in what non-profits a foundation gave to, for what purposes, and when. The Johnson Amendment explicitly prohibits non-profits from endorsing political candidates, giving them contributions, or campaigning for them.

Laws That Affect Relationships Between Donors and Non-profits

The IRS has ruled that when a donor makes a charitable gift, they must completely let go of all ownership of the gift if it is to be considered tax deductible. The donor cannot receive anything of value in return for his charitable gift, i.e., no quid pro quo. An example would be that a board member cannot be given a contract to sell goods or services to the charity when they make a large gift to the non-profit. There is a rule that applies to when a donor can be credited for a gift. When the donor mails it or when the non-profit receives it? The IRS considers that a donor has let go of control of a gift on the day their contribution envelope is postmarked. That's why gifts opened at the charity on January 2, for example, can be credited to the donor for the preceding year for tax purposes if the postmark was made in December. The same is true for stock gifts. The date it is credited is the date the broker made the wire transfer. In the planned giving realm, the non-profit must record the value of a bequest as revenue on the date an attorney notifies a charity that a donor has died and left the charity a specific amount in their will. The money will flow in later, but the gift must be recorded at the date of notification.

Laws That Affect Fundraising Staff and Donors

Pledging is the prime legal issue between staff and donors. An oral pledge means nothing. A written pledge is a contract the donor signs to guarantee payment, now or by a specified date in the future. Non-profits have gone to court to have pledges enforced. Another issue is a challenge to a bequest by family members. Sometimes when a donor dies and leaves a large sum of money to a non-profit, the family will fight it. If the bequest is large enough to make a difference, the non-profit will sue in court to receive it. What grounds do families attempt to use to fight a bequest? If the donor's intent was (A) and now the intended recipient—a department or a program or a library—no longer exists, the family will want the bequest declared null and void. However, it's a difficult case to make because large non-profits will argue that, even if the intended recipient program or department (A) no longer exists, there are very similar programs (B) that would benefit.

94

Fundraising Laws That Affect Staff and Prospects

All states follow federal laws concerning fundraising, but many states require charities to register with the state in order to do business. The states' main concern is preventing unscrupulous organizations from defrauding citizens. Within this issue of fraud is the question of where does someone's charitable gift go. The states urge citizens to thoroughly research a non-profit before making a gift. Individuals can turn to GuideStar online to check the viability of many non-profits. If a charity spends a great deal of money to raise funds, should that be a red flag? Maybe, but it's not illegal. Individuals should make their own judgments about the ratio of money raised to the money spent on expenses. There are no laws preventing non-profits from spending enormous sums on fundraising expenses. In fact, this activity is protected by the First Amendment.

Legal and Ethical Practices

Related to Donor Record Maintenance

The IRS stipulates that a donor must receive a receipt from a non-profit for a gift of $250 or more for the gift to be tax deductible. Non-profits must have a donor database to record all gifts in order to send receipts at the time of the gift or later when a donor asks for one. It's common for donors to request duplicates of their gift receipts months later when they prepare their income tax forms. Non-profits will send a receipt showing the name of the non-profit, the non-profit's address, the date of the gift, the amount, what form it took (check, cash, credit card, or wire transfer), and the name or names it was credited to. Some non-profits make photocopies of checks received, cash, credit card information, and proof of wire transfer. However, non-profits should be scrupulous about redacting most of the credit card numbers to prevent theft and fraud. Cash donations are sensitive because of the possibility of theft, so gift accountants should make photocopies and have their steps witnessed and verified by coworkers. Non-profits should keep appraisals of the value of gifts in kind, and donors are responsible for getting appraisals and paying for them.

Related to Gift Accounting

The Financial Accounting Standards Board (FASB) has stated that gifts received by non-profits should be classified as unrestricted, temporarily restricted, or permanently restricted. Non-profits will be able to classify gifts based on the wishes of donors. FASB also has said that written pledges will be recognized as revenue for the non-profit. As the non-profit carries these written pledges on their books, they will be subject to discounts. Because pledges are counted as revenue, it's important that non-profits keep track of pledges, remind the individual who pledged of their pledged amount, and ask for fulfillment. The frequency of reminders is up to the non-profit, and it will have to decide what is best. Non-profits have to be very careful about classifying gifts correctly because the classifications are reflected in a non-profit's statement of assets. FASB has rules that determine how these asset values change based on how the gifts are classified.

Related to Financial Management and Audit Trails

An audit trail is a full documentation of a charitable gift, from its receipt to its entry into the database to its deposit in the non-profit's bank, into which and how it is pooled with other gifts to pay bills or meet a payroll. It will show a copy of the receipt sent to the donor. When a donor makes a gift of stock, the audit trail will show when the stock gift was wired, from whom, when it went into the non-profit's DTC account, how it was valued on the day it was received, how it was sold, and when the proceeds were deposited into the non-profit's account. Accounting departments will be able to show automatic paper trails using recommended software. A non-profit's management should be consistently transparent with its finances. Its financial reports to the board of directors, its annual 990 filing, the annual report to donors and other constituents, the budget it sends to

95

foundations, and the financial statements it presents to banks when applying for a loan should reveal everything financially related. Financial transparency will maintain the non-profit's integrity in the community.

Recording Charitable Gifts

Small non-profits starting out may use Excel spreadsheets, but they will likely migrate their data to a database that features customer relationship management software before long. Non-profits will record the gifts they receive by creating records in the database for each donor. They will populate each record with as much as they know about the donor, including address, title, employer, ratings, matching gift, the development director assigned to the donor, last visit, a link to call reports from visits, the next visit due date, the names of the donor's family and friends, alma mater and degree(s), estimated net worth, and a code showing them as a planned giving prospect.

Receiving and Acknowledging Gifts

Most non-profits will send out letters of thanks to donors within a very short amount of time. Prompt acknowledgments are very important to show donors appreciation and thank them for their thoughtfulness. If donors are not thanked promptly, or not thanked at all, they are not likely to donate again because they didn't sense their gifts were needed. The best acknowledgment letters to large donors include a hand-written note at the top from the CEO. They should be sent first class, not bulk, and the letters always should include a business reply envelope for the donor's next donation. The donor's name, address, and salutation should be perfect, or donors will think the non-profit is careless and failed to get their details right, which is often the case. When a gift is received from a corporation or foundation, the non-profit should send a letter of thanks to their contact. When a bequest is received, the non-profit should write an acknowledgment letter to the attorney and the executor of the estate. It's smart to include brochures with letters to third parties because it's unlikely they will be familiar with the non-profit. Attorneys and executors will notify the non-profit if members of the decedent's family also should be acknowledged.

Recognizing Charitable Gifts

Non-profits use traditional methods to recognize charitable gifts because donors have come to expect them. When a non-profit prints its annual or quarterly magazine, donors expect to see their names on an honor roll. They expect the non-profit to spell their names correctly and to list their names at the correct giving level. Universities and independent schools can name scholarships after donors who designate their gifts for financial aid. Sometimes scholarship donors name their scholarships in memory of relatives or esteemed faculty members. These donors expect the scholarship names to be spelled correctly as well as their own names. Donors who make principal gifts allow non-profits to name buildings for them. They expect to receive this kind of honor when they make gifts of $1 million and more, and they expect their names to be spelled correctly. Recognition also comes in the form of honoring donors during black tie dinners when their peers are in attendance. Awards ceremonies call special attention to one donor who has made significant gifts. Of course, recognition is the ultimate form of cultivation, and the more special the honor, the more meaningful the cultivation.

Gift Acceptance Policies

Without a gift acceptance policy, a non-profit is liable to accept anything it is offered and that can and will lead to problems the agency is better off without. It helps a development officer say, "I'm sorry, we can't accept that, it's against our policy" when a gift-in-kind donor wants to give something that's not useful or so complex it will eat up a great deal of staff time. It also injects some discipline into the process and provides rules for being consistent. A non-profit doesn't want to get the reputation for taking anything that's offered, or it will be inundated with useless gifts. For useful transactions, a gift acceptance policy will describe in detail how cash is to be handled, how stock that is wired to the non-profit's DTC account will be processed, how trusts and annuities will be handled, and if the organization will accept real estate or life insurance. If members of the board of directors discuss the gift acceptance policies, they too will become familiar with what is useful and what isn't, which might give them pause when they have an idea to donate something impractical.

Benefits of Gift Agreements

A charitable gift agreement, if written correctly, serves as a contract between a donor who makes a pledge and the charity that receives it. The donor agrees to give the charity a specified amount of money by a certain date, and the charity agrees to accept payment for the pledge in one lump sum, in annual payments, in cash, or with stock (but not gifts in kind). If the donor expects their employer to match their gift, this also should be declared. It is the donor's responsibility to file matching gift forms with their employer. A pledge is legally enforceable, and the non-profit may sue to recover the pledge amount. If the donor pledges a gift to a special restricted fund or wants a building named for them, their gift deposited into the endowment, or their gift used to pay down a debt or a mortgage on a building, then the gift agreement guarantees the non-profit will follow their wishes. If, in later years, the non-profit wants to abandon the donor's wish and move the money for some other purpose, the donor must give their permission. If the donor is dead, the non-profit must seek out permission from the family.

Accounting Principles for Non-profits

A perplexing problem for many non-profits is this: Why don't the financial reports from accounting agree with the reports from development? This situation happens often when both the comptroller and the development director present different totals for the year to the board of directors. This occurs regularly and it's confusing for everyone involved. Basically, the problem is how charitable gifts are entered into both departments' computers. For example, the development office accounting method is a cash system. It records every pledge payment as cash is deposited. The accounting department uses the accrual method, and it records the full amount in the year the pledge was made, even if the payments may not come in for months or years. Why the difference? The accounting department must follow the generally accepted accounting principles that mandate accrual accounting.

Investment Principles for Non-profits

Members of the board of directors for non-profits have what is commonly called a fiduciary responsibility to protect the organization's assets. Before they undertake any investment decisions, however, they should write an investment policy. This policy will determine how much risk the board is willing to take with its investments: How much cash it wants to have liquid, how much it's willing to put into fixed income investments, and how much it's willing to invest for the long term. Most boards of directors don't involve themselves in day-to-day decisions about buying stocks and bonds and other investment instruments. They hire an investment manager and tell them broadly how they want the non-profit's accounts invested. Once a year they can review how well the manager has performed and determine if they want to leave the investments with them or change managers and leave their investment policy intact or revise it.

Non-profit Organizational Transparency

The IRS requires non-profits to complete and file form 990, which outlines important details about how the organization operates: all revenues going back five years and broken down by source, total assets, biggest expenditures for services and events, the names of all of the board members, the highest paid staff and their salaries and deferred compensation, detailed descriptions of the mission and how it is carried out, and specific investment instruments and their value at the time the form is completed. Many non-profits produce and distribute annual reports with photos and detailed narratives about the clients they serve, new programs, acknowledgments and photos of volunteers and volunteer groups, revenue, grants received, charitable gifts received, photos of events, logos of corporations that are supportive, photos of the CEO and board chair, and link to the website.

Reporting Fundraising Performance

Form 990 that non-profits file with the IRS breaks down the fundraising totals for each of the past five years; the sources of the funds including grants, individual contributions, and events; and readers can see if gifts have steadily increased, decreased, or remain static. Some universities annually produce honor rolls of donors, and the names and the charitable gifts they gave are listed. Most non-profits print capital campaign reports that show fundraising progress to date toward the goal, with the names of individuals and foundations that have made major gift commitments to components of the campaign. When foundations make grant commitments, they sometimes mandate that the non-profit raise equal amounts. To receive the matching grant, the non-profits must report their own fundraising results.

Reporting Outcomes and Impacts on Constituencies

Many non-profits produce and distribute annual reports with photos and detailed narratives about the clients they serve. Annual reports tell stories about individual people and their circumstances; detailed descriptions of their problems; how they were evaluated by social workers; what therapies, programs, and other services were prescribed; their progress; and how their lives improved. Newsletters accomplish the same things but in a shorter format. When non-profits apply for grants from foundations, the foundations' program officers will specify the kinds of outcomes they anticipate and how the non-profits will measure them. If non-profits receive money from the United Way, they have to file similar reports showing outcomes. Every non-profit's website may resemble their annual reports in the ways in which they portray their successes with the people they serve. Non-profits hold annual galas to thank donors and to present their success stories to a large group of interested attendees. It's common practice for these non-profits to invite some of the people they serve to speak. They talk about their lives and predicaments, how the professional people in the agency helped them, and the progress they have made. Testimonials like these can inspire donors to continue their support and prospects to consider becoming involved.

The Donor Bill of Rights (as developed by AAFRC, AHP, CASE, and AFP)

Philanthropy is based on voluntary action for the common good. It is a tradition of giving and sharing that is primary to the quality of life. To ensure that philanthropy merits the respect and trust of the general public, and that donors and prospective donors can have full confidence in the not-for-profit organizations and causes they are asked to support, we declare that all donors have these rights:

- To be informed of the organization's mission, of the way the organization intends to use donated resources, and of its capacity to use donations effectively for their intended purposes.
- To be informed of the identity of those serving on the organization's governing board, and to expect the board to exercise prudent judgment in its stewardship responsibilities.
- To have access to the organization's most recent financial statements.
- To be assured their gifts will be used for the purposes for which they were given.
- To receive appropriate acknowledgement and recognition.
- To be assured that information about their donation is handled with respect and with confidentiality to the extent provided by law.
- To expect that all relationships with individuals representing organizations of interest to the donor will be professional in nature.
- To be informed whether those seeking donations are volunteers, employees of the organization, or hired solicitors.
- To have the opportunity for their names to be deleted from mailing lists that an organization may intend to share.
- To feel free to ask questions when making a donation and to receive prompt, truthful, and forthright answers.

Protection of Donors' Personal Information

Among non-profits there has been a practice in the past of swapping donor mailing lists with other non-profits. The practice has been a common one in the past. Non-profits have sold their mailing lists to other non-profits as well as commercial list brokers. Donors may not be aware of this practice and they probably wouldn't continue to operate this way if their donors found out. When they receive calls and letters from charities they don't know, they may figure it out anyway. Some donors ask non-profits to list their gifts as "Anonymous" in donor lists for this reason. The best practice is (1) for charities not to sell their mailing lists and (2) to tell their donors that their personal information is private and will not be sold to anyone. Non-profits should post this kind of notice on their websites, in their direct mail, in their annual reports, and in telemarketing inserts to reassure donors and prospective donors of complete privacy.

Ethical Principles and Unethical Practices

Cultivating Gifts

When a development officer talks about charitable gift annuities, for example, they should not mislead a prospective donor. They should not tell a donor that a CGA is an investment because it is not. A CGA is a charitable gift that provides lifetime income, and while some of the income is tax free, some is taxable. A CGA also is an irrevocable instrument, unlike a true investment. Development officers should be honest and clear about what a bequest will accomplish and what it may not. At the time it is signed, a bequest may appear to be large enough to earn naming rights to a building. However, if a significant number of years goes by between the year of the signing and the year of the donor's death, it may no longer qualify. Along those same lines, it may not be ethical for a development officer to promise to use a donor's bequest to support specific programming in the future. For example, if a college for Catholic girls accepted a bequest to support a scholarship for Catholic girls only 50 years ago, the requirement may become irrelevant if the college becomes nonsectarian. It may be both unethical and illegal to restrict the award to a specific gender and religion. The lesson is for the development officer to never make promises that are half-truths or impossible to keep after the passage of time.

<u>Securing Gifts</u>

A development officer might promise a donor that their gift is tax deductible when it is not. For example, non-profits that do not have 501(c)(3) approval from the IRS cannot legally say all gifts to their organization are tax deductible. This obviously is unethical. The ethical thing to say is that the gift is not deductible but that there are other non-profits that perform the same work. A development officer might say that it is unnecessary for a donor to call their lawyer to discuss the viability of a planned gift. This is unethical. Donors always should be encouraged to seek an attorney's help if they have questions or doubts, particularly when the subject is income tax. It is unethical for a charity to steer donors to specific attorneys. Development officers may offer a list of attorneys that have treated their donors well in the past, and let the donors choose. It is unethical for a development officer to seek out and accept a percentage of the money they raise. To correct any misunderstanding, a development officer may tell a donor that, in the interest of full disclosure, they are not earning commission from the formation of the gift. A member of the board of directors may not benefit personally from fundraising activities.

Ethical Decision Making

If a non-profit has outlined its gift acceptance policies, has developed a donor bill of rights, a set of bylaws, policies for finance, and other control measures, it then has a set of rules and regulations it can refer to when problematic situations arise. For example, if a board member presents an offer to make a charitable gift that will benefit him but won't benefit the non-profit, the organization can refuse and point to its rules forbidding conflicts of interest as the reason why. When a bequest comes in for the support of a specific purpose that no longer exists at the organization, the surviving family sometimes sues. When that happens, the charity may sue the family to receive the bequest because it's for the benefit of the mission and the people they serve. To sue, in this case, is an ethical decision. Sometimes a donor inquires about buying a charitable gift annuity and wants to arrange for one that's so large that the charity doesn't see a way to make payments to the donor for life. Rather than refuse the gift, the ethical thing to do would be to arrange for a large affiliated non-profit foundation to take the annuity, make payments to the donor, and then donate the corpus back to the original non-profit after the donor dies.

Continuing Education

The following are some professional organizations where development directors can continue their education:

- Association of Fundraising Professionals (AFP). AFP provides webinars, courses, a leadership academy, and national conferences to help development professionals learn more skills.
- National Association of Charitable Gift Planners (NACGP). Produces courses, conferences, and conventions to teach development directors more about planned giving.
- Local planned giving councils. Development professionals can attend monthly meetings locally to hear speakers, ask questions, and network with other development directors.
- Council for the Advancement and Support of Education (CASE). CASE provides training, books, articles, and conferences primarily for development officers who work for universities, colleges, and independent schools.

Finding Mentors and Becoming a Mentor

Conventional wisdom says that one-on-one mentoring is much better than sending young people to conferences and courses, buying books, or attending webinars. There is much to learn in development and learning it from a seasoned professional makes a significant difference. Some AFP chapters promote one-on-one mentoring programs that offer young people the chance to be mentored by senior development directors with at least 15 years of experience. For the most part, it's a better practice for young people to seek out their own mentors.

Benefits from Being Involved on Professional Committees

The most significant benefit that can come from joining a professional committee is finding new mentors. Professional committees at groups like AFP are made up of a diverse set of professionals from higher education, social services, food pantries, religious bodies, art museums, and other local organizations. Young people can find natural mentors on these committees, and they can learn about professional opportunities.

Learning About Research

Several cities have opened centers for philanthropy that maintain information about their areas' philanthropic landscape. They offer free resources to learn about, among other things, prospect research for individuals, foundations, and corporations. They explain community foundations where donor-advised funds can be found, and that have available a common grant application.

Mentorship Principles

Mentors should create some boundaries for their time with mentees and make them known to them. Mentees should guide the conversation, asking mentors to explain things they've only been slightly exposed to before. Mentors should not confuse mentoring with assigning mentees tasks. Mentors should be teaching by example, modeling the kind of strategies that are effective. Mentees can demonstrate professional progress to their mentors and ask for feedback. Some mentoring sources recommend that a mentoring relationship have an end date. Others believe that mentoring is ongoing teaching and should continue indefinitely as long as both parties agree.

Professional Associations Supporting Advocacy

The Association of Fundraising Professionals (AFP) encourages and supports advocacy for people who work in development and fundraising. AFP produces extensive educational materials and conferences.

Council for the Advancement and Support of Education (CASE) produces and distributes educational materials for development professionals who work for universities and independent schools. CASE produces regional and national conferences.

National Association of Charitable Gift Planners (NACGP) is one of several national organizations that promotes the profession of planned giving. Local and regional planned giving councils are very useful for professionals who are looking for continuing education.

Helpful Avenues for Advocacy

Successful non-profits are continuously making friends and putting those friends to work for them in the community. Members of the board of directors should know enough about the non-profit to talk about its mission and accomplishments with friends and in social settings. Every time someone new hears positive things from a friend they trust, the chances increase that they might become supporters. Universities can appoint loyal alumni as ambassadors in their communities to initiate positive conversations about their alma maters in their communities. Often small social services agencies will band together to advocate for social change. The strategy there is that media might pay attention to a large group advocating, where they might ignore a small one. This group advocacy also frequently takes the form of lobbying. A non-profit group can hire a lobbyist to make their case in a state legislature.

CFRE Practice Test

1. What does the term "two-life charitable gift annuity (CGA)" mean?

    a. The donor buys a CGA for himself and his spouse.
    b. The CGA payout will be determined by the annuitants' ages.
    c. The CGA payout goes to both annuitants simultaneously.
    d. When the donor dies, payments to his spouse will stop.

2. A major gift solicitation plan begins with finding what crucial piece of information in an individual's file?

    a. A report on the donor's stock holdings gleaned from the Securities and Exchange Commission's Electronic Data Gathering, Analysis, and Retrieval (EDGAR) database
    b. A development officer rating the donor as "qualified"
    c. A copy of the pages from his will that describe a bequest designated for the nonprofit
    d. A code that screening and rating software has provided

3. What best describes a bequest?

    a. Irrevocable
    b. A gift of privately held stock
    c. Revocable
    d. A verbal agreement

4. Does a donor receive credit for his or her gift when the nonprofit opens the envelope containing his check?

    a. Yes, the nonprofit has to receive the gift to give credit for it.
    b. No, the donor's date of gift is the postmark on the envelope.
    c. Yes, the nonprofit is required to stamp it with the date when they open it, and that is the date the gift is given.
    d. No, the nonprofit has to deposit it in the bank before any credit is given.

5. What do the acronyms LYBUNT and SYBUNT stand for?

    a. Last Year But Unfortunately Not This and Some Year in the past But Unfortunately Not This—they are annual fund vocabulary words.
    b. Liabilities listed by Year in all Bonded Unified Non-Grantor Trusts and Securities listed by Year in Base currency in a Unified Non-Grantee Trust—nonprofits have to see investments in trusts.
    c. Liquid Yield Bond Uniform Noncompliance Tax and Scheduled Yield Bond Uniform Noncompliance Tax—noncompliance taxes lower the values of bonds.
    d. List Your Baseline Unitrusts and their Net Transaction exposure and Schedule Your Baseline Unitrusts and their Net Transaction exposure—exposure indicates legal vulnerabilities.

6. When a capital campaign manager begins to assemble a plan to reach a campaign goal, what is one instrument he or she can use to illustrate what gifts will be needed?

    a. A gift table
    b. A timeline
    c. A construction schedule with named gift opportunities
    d. A pie chart showing sources of funding

7. What term refers to an individual who becomes the subject of wealth research but is not yet assigned to a development officer?

    a. A prospect
    b. A suspect
    c. A target
    d. A partially identified subject

8. What should the donor recognition page of a nonprofit's website always include?

    a. All donors' names and the giving categories they fall into
    b. A mechanism to make a stock transfer online
    c. Photos of the gifts a donor can receive from the nonprofit
    d. A threshold for giving-level recognition

9. When a donor's stockbroker or wealth advisor calls to notify the development office that his or her client is sending a stock or bond gift electronically, what are the most important questions to ask?

    a. What is your client's name? What is the name of the company that issued the stock?
    b. What is the value of the stock? Is that its value today?
    c. What is your firm's account number? What bank do you use?
    d. What was the value of the stock when your client bought it? What year did he or she buy it?

10. When a donor expresses a desire to create a trust so the nonprofit will be included, who should write the trust document?

    a. The development officer with the trust officer
    b. The development officer with the donor's attorney
    c. The donor's attorney
    d. The donor's accountant with the family's approval

11. What is meant by the term "soft credit?"

    a. Soft credit means that a donor has made a gift and the nonprofit is waiting for the matching gift from his or her employer.
    b. When a donor makes a gift and says that it is also from his or her spouse, the nonprofit gives the spouse soft credit.
    c. A donor who gave in the past is put on the soft credit list because the nonprofit assumes he or she will give again this year.
    d. When a foundation gives a capital gift to a nonprofit only when it meets its campaign goal, the gift is called soft credit.

12. After visiting a prospect, how much speculation can a development director use in his or her call report?

    a. When a development director surmises that a prospect has been married several times, he or she should make a note so the nonprofit is aware of the prospect's financial obligations.
    b. A development director should not speculate.
    c. If a development director feels certain that a donor has told the truth about another donor's legal problems, it's pertinent information that belongs in the file.
    d. If a prospect is related to a wealthy donor, the development director can assume that the prospect can make a large gift.

13. How often should a development office check for updated addresses and phone numbers for its donors?
   a. Every year
   b. Every five years
   c. Every ten years
   d. Whenever a mailer is returned by the post office

14. What is the program for updating addresses called?
   a. National Change of Address (NCOA)
   b. Open Addresses (OA)
   c. National Address Database (NAD)
   d. National Address Schema (NAS)

15. If a donor has undergone gender reassignment, what gender do you use in his or her file in the donor database?
   a. Gender codes are not used in the database.
   b. You use whatever the donor tells you to use.
   c. Use the gender code from the donor's tax return.
   d. It is illegal to identify a person's gender without permission.

16. What is form 990, and why is it useful?
   a. It is a tax return all nonprofits put online for everyone to access.
   b. It's a form nonprofits use that reveals their income, expenses, the highest salaries of their administrators, their board members' names, and total revenues for the last five years.
   c. It lists all of the nonprofit's donors and their donation amounts, including individuals and foundations.
   d. It is a planned giving form that is used to calculate the return of a charitable gift annuity.

17. Is part of the income from a charitable gift annuity a piece of the donor's original principal that is returned?
   a. Yes, but during some years he or she might not receive a payment.
   b. No, the nonprofit invests all of the principal and the annuitant receives profits from the investment.
   c. Yes, that is why part of a charitable gift annuity payment is not taxable.
   d. No, it is illegal to tell a donor that he or she will receive some money back.

18. When a donor makes a gift in honor of a friend, and the nonprofit notifies the friend of this honor, what should be included in the notification?
   a. The name of the donor
   b. The name of the donor and the amount of the gift
   c. No notification of the honoree necessary
   d. A gift envelope for the honoree to use to match the donor's gift

19. How are the rates for charitable gift annuities determined?
   a. They are determined by the American Council on Gift Annuities.
   b. The Internal Revenue Service sets the rates annually.
   c. They are determined by the Federal Reserve Board.
   d. They parallel current bank loan interest rates.

20. Should all nonprofits use the same rates when they run calculations for donors who may be interested in a charitable gift annuity?

   a. No, they are a guide, but nonprofits may exercise their own judgments about what they can afford.
   b. Yes, the rates are established for all nonprofits so the playing field is level.
   c. No, nonprofits can offer all kinds of incentives for donors to buy their charitable gift annuities.
   d. Yes, donors use the same rates, but they can use different online annuity calculators to derive different scenarios.

21. Before a nonprofit accepts a gift of a painting, what must be done?

   a. The nonprofit must get the art appraised to determine its value.
   b. The nonprofit must line up a buyer for the art so it can sell it.
   c. The donors must arrange for an art appraisal and pay for it.
   d. Calculations must be run to determine what tax deduction the painter can take.

22. If a nonprofit's advisory board has no real power to govern and set policy, why is it important to do the staff work to maintain the board's activities?

   a. An advisory board gives management a chance to observe how committed its members are and evaluate their leadership skills. The best board members can be elevated to the board of trustees.
   b. Advisory board members can deduct their board service time from their income taxes.
   c. All advisory board members are paid to serve. If they give their payments back to the nonprofit, they can take generous tax deductions.
   d. To maintain their accreditation status, every nonprofit must have an advisory board and keep records of the minutes.

23. When a donor makes a gift of life insurance to a nonprofit, may he or she deduct the premiums paid to keep the policy active?

   a. No, the premiums are paid by the insured to the insurance company so the nonprofit is not involved.
   b. Yes, the nonprofit is the donor's beneficiary.
   c. Yes, and the donor also may deduct the value of the insurance policy's payoff.
   d. Yes, if the donor sends the premium to the nonprofit, and the nonprofit makes the donor's premium payment.

24. Why are some nonprofits reluctant to recognize the gifts of life insurance policies in capital campaign totals?

   a. Donors do not always provide proof that they have the policies or proof of their value.
   b. A donor can switch the policy's beneficiary from the nonprofit to a relative or to anyone else at any time.
   c. If the donor takes out a life insurance policy as a gift, the company might go out of business and the nonprofit won't receive the payout.
   d. Most are not reluctant to recognize an insurance gift.

25. If a donor only gives $10 per year but has made that gift every year for 20 years, what might that indicate?

    a. It indicates the donor is consistently loyal to the nonprofit, and that loyalty might indicate he or she is able and willing to make a larger gift.

    b. The donor probably cannot afford more than a $10 gift, but he or she wants to participate and see his or her name on the donor rolls.

    c. The donor might split annual giving between several nonprofits, dividing the total amount into equal gifts.

    d. It indicates the donor isn't generous and the nonprofit should not spend much time with him or her.

26. What source of funding is the largest for a nonprofit?

    a. Corporate giving

    b. Foundation giving

    c. Individual giving

    d. Federated giving

27. When a donor sets up a trust to pay income to a charity for a specified number of years, what is that trust called?

    a. A charitable lead trust

    b. A charitable remainder trust

    c. A charitable annuity trust

    d. A charitable annuity trust with makeup provisions

28. When a nonprofit holds a phonathon and a worker calls a donor who says he or she is on the No Call List and that he or she will report the nonprofit, what does the organization need to do?

    a. Tell the donor a development director will call the next day and straighten everything out.

    b. Nothing—charities are exempt from the No Call List but may code the donor's file "no calls."

    c. Apologize and buy a new No Call List.

    d. Tell the donor that he or she will not receive any more phone calls or mail from the charity.

29. Some employers make it clear they will not match their employees' gifts to what kind of organization?

    a. Environmental

    b. Educational

    c. Religious

    d. Social services

30. In nonprofit organizations, what does the term "participation rate" mean?"

    a. The participation rate is a measurement of the annual fund's effectiveness; at a university, it measures what percent of the total alumni base gave in a specific year.

    b. In many organizations that are staffed by volunteers, the participation rate is a measurement of how many volunteers worked out of the total number of volunteers in the database.

    c. The participation rate is calculated by quoting the percentage of donors that gave this year compared with how many gave last year.

    d. When nonprofits record pledges, the participation rate is calculated by comparing how many pledges converted to paid gifts.

31. In terms of total charitable giving in the United States, how do baby boomer women compare with people in other demographics?
    a. Baby boomer women who are retired are much more cautious with their money.
    b. Baby boomer men are paid more than women, so their charitable giving is much higher.
    c. Baby boomer women give as much as baby boomer men.
    d. Baby boomer women give much more than baby boomer men.

32. What does a nonprofit mean when it quotes its average gift?
    a. The calculation of an average gift is the total dollars in annual contributions divided by the number of gifts received.
    b. The average gift is the median level of giving throughout the nonprofit's history.
    c. It means whatever amount a corporation gives at a certain level of sponsorship in a normal year.
    d. Average giving is relative—what may seem like a generous gift to some nonprofits is a major gift to others.

33. How do donors avoid paying capital gains taxes on stock they have owned for a long time?
    a. They instruct their brokers to sell it and then send the proceeds to a nonprofit.
    b. They transfer ownership of the stock to a nonprofit.
    c. They put the stock that has increased in value into their wills and pass it on to their heirs.
    d. They convert the stock to preferred shares and sell it when the company is sold.

34. When companies and the federal government ask their employees to pledge donations for charity, what are these annual campaigns called?
    a. Payroll and federated campaigns
    b. The United Way
    c. Giving Tuesdays
    d. GoFundMe

35. What is the difference between fund-raising and philanthropy?
    a. A fund-raiser enables participants to take immediate tax deductions. Philanthropy makes tax deductions more long range.
    b. They are almost the same thing. The word "fund-raising" is used as a term when people are raising cash; "philanthropy" is used when people are generous with their time.
    c. Fund-raising means money coming in. Philanthropy means money going out.
    d. Fund-raising is often an emotional reaction to a natural disaster or other different, immediate needs. Philanthropy is a sustained effort to build and improve a nonprofit's programs and structures.

36. Does the board of directors manage or govern a nonprofit?
    a. A board governs a nonprofit, and the staff manages a nonprofit's operations.
    b. A board manages a nonprofit because it is responsible for its programmatic capabilities, financial stability, and maintenance of accreditation.
    c. A board both governs and manages a nonprofit because it's common for a nonprofit's leaders not to have management training.
    d. The board approves all hires, expenditures, fee-based revenues, new leases, and taxes.

37. What is the LEAST effective way for a nonprofit to acquire new donors?

    a. When a nonprofit holds events its development directors meet new people and attempt to gauge their interests.
    b. A nonprofit can ask current donors to recommend some new suspects.
    c. Nonprofits can acquire thousands of names by purchasing mailing lists.
    d. Some of the best new donors are previous donors who stopped donating at some point.

38. Is there a way for a nonprofit to establish standards for what charitable gifts it will and will not accept?

    a. Yes, a nonprofit's board can write a set of gift acceptance policies to protect the charity from gifts it does not want or cannot handle.
    b. No, the Internal Revenue Service clearly has set these standards, and it issues new addendum.
    c. Yes, the development office can look at what gifts have and have not been accepted in the past and make decisions according to historical standards.
    d. No, the Federal Accounting Standards Board has strict rules that nonprofits must follow.

39. At a charity event, how much of an individual's auction and gambling winnings are tax deductible?

    a. All winnings are tax deductible.
    b. None are tax deductible.
    c. Auction winnings are tax deductible, but gambling winnings are not.
    d. Only 50 percent of auction and gambling winnings would be tax deductible.

40. What is the conventional wisdom about people who leave bequests for nonprofits in their wills?

    a. They are not capable of making large outright gifts.
    b. They use bequests as an excuse not to make annual gifts.
    c. Nonprofits can receive much more from bequests from some donors than they will ever receive from outright giving.
    d. Nonprofits can't depend on bequests from donors.

41. What two characteristics indicate that an individual could be a good prospect for a charitable gift?

    a. A high standing in the community and a known millionaire
    b. The capacity to give and an inclination to give
    c. Living in a zip code where wealthy people live and appearing frequently in photos of charitable events
    d. Attending all of the nonprofit's events and frequent volunteering

42. What does the term "moves management" mean?

    a. It means setting up a system to update donors' addresses when they change residences.
    b. In development, the term "moves" means donors move up from one recognized giving level to another. Managing it means tracking the changes in levels.
    c. For universities in which the registrar and development use the same software, moves management means migrating graduated students into the alumni database.
    d. Development directors move donors and prospects through cultivation levels to develop closer relationships with the nonprofit. Managing the moves means setting up the process strategically.

43. What important details about a donor cannot be extracted from the donor database by screening software?

    a. The value of assets in a trust in the donor's name
    b. The amount of stock he or she owns and its value
    c. The property ownership and its value
    d. Major gifts he or she has made to other nonprofits

44. What impact does race have on a donor's generosity?

    a. African Americans have traditionally given more than other races.
    b. Asian Americans give less than other races.
    c. Race makes no difference in donors' giving rates.
    d. Hispanic donors give less than whites but more than African Americans.

45. Who assigns donors and prospects to staff in a development office?

    a. The development officers, vice president, prospect researchers, and database coordinator make the assignments as a group.
    b. The CEO or president chooses donors and prospects, and the rest are unassigned.
    c. The vice president assigns all donors and prospects.
    d. The prospect researcher makes the assignments based on staff contacts documented in the database.

46. What happens at the end of a fiscal year when a donor fails to pay an annual pledge?

    a. The nonprofit keeps reminding the donor in succeeding years.
    b. The donor is removed from the next round of solicitations because he or she can't be counted on.
    c. If it is an annual fund pledge that goes unpaid, it is cancelled in the database.
    d. The donor's name is printed in a "dishonor roll."

47. What can a nonprofit do if a large, unwritten pledge to a capital campaign goes unpaid?

    a. Nothing—donors have the legal right to not pay a pledge if they change their minds.
    b. A nonprofit can sue for payment because a capital pledge is considered a contract, and it is legally enforceable.
    c. It can negotiate a smaller pledge and create an easier payment schedule.
    d. A capital pledge is considered an account receivable, and a nonprofit will add interest and penalties to unpaid pledges.

48. If a donor leaves a bequest for a specific restricted purpose and, after the donor's death, the purpose no longer exists, can the nonprofit use the bequest for something else?

    a. No, bequests are legal documents that were written to be followed to the letter of the law.
    b. Sometimes, but it depends on the language of the bequest and the donor's family.
    c. No, because funds cannot be comingled.
    d. Yes, because the donor is deceased.

49. What is a strong behavioral habit development officers can cultivate that can help establish strong relationships with donors?

    a. Be honest about how you feel about management's major decisions to show solidarity.

    b. When donors ask if other people gave as much as they did, tell them so they know they're not alone in their support.

    c. Never gossip with donors; they must trust you implicitly.

    d. Offer major naming opportunities to donors in an upcoming capital building plan.

50. What is the best response to a community member who asks a development officer about programs that are no longer offered or an original mission that has evolved over the decades?

    a. It's important to correct the individual right away and explain that the community has misunderstood the nonprofit for decades.

    b. Relay the individual's misunderstandings to the public relations staff so they can begin to discuss how they can create messages that reflect the nonprofit's current mission and services.

    c. Listen to their concerns carefully, and promise to get back to them with explanations.

    d. Explain that the nonprofit's original mission is no longer relevant to current circumstances and needs.

Answer Key and Explanations

1. A: An annuity buyer can purchase a single-life annuity for him- or herself. The buyer will be paid in installments, and when he or she dies, the charity keeps the principal. A buyer also can purchase an annuity for him- or herself and his or her spouse, and it's called a two-life annuity. The other answers are incorrect because they don't speak to the specific definition of a two-life charitable gift annuity (CGA).

2. B: If the individual has been "qualified," the development staff has decided that the individual has a strong propensity for charitable giving, your nonprofit is his priority, and he or she has the wealth to make a major gift.

3. C: A bequest can be changed at any time. Nonprofits may take a bequest through a process of discounting, which seeks to place a present-day value on the gift that will come in the future.

4. B: The donor's date of gift is the postmark on his envelope. The general principle is the date that the donor relinquishes control of the charitable donation is the date of the gift. Placing a check in an envelope and mailing it is considered relinquishing control. The postmark on the envelope proves the date when he should be credited. This is very important to donors who mail their gifts on or before December 31.

5. A: These acronyms are used to write code for the database to sort and produce direct mail lists. LYBUNT means Last Year But Unfortunately Not This. The list will contain the names of donors who gave last year but not yet this year. SYBUNT means Some Year But Unfortunately Not This. This list will contain the names of donors who gave sometime in the past or some year but not this year yet. PYBUNT means Past Year But Unfortunately Not This. Specifically, the term "past year" means two years ago. These acronyms are important only when a nonprofit is segmenting its direct mail. For example, a LYBUNT letter may say, for example, "Thank you for your gift of $50 last year. Unfortunately, we haven't heard from you yet this year."

6. A: A campaign manager creates a gift table that shows how many gifts at each dollar level will be needed to meet the goal.

7. B: The development office suspects an individual is a prospect but doesn't know yet that it is true. The information backing this up is only conjecture. A suspect converts to a prospect when conjecture turns into solid facts.

8. A: Most nonprofits print an annual donor list to recognize generous people that support them. (

9. A: Many gifts come in by wire transfer without the donor's name and the name of the stock. The stockbroker should identify the client and the name of the stock.

10. C: A development officer should be very clear that writing a trust document should be done by the donor's attorney. Development officers generally are not practicing attorneys. If they are law school graduates, they still should advise a donor to hire his or her own counsel to work on the donor's behalf. This prevents any appearance of manipulation. Development officers may not suggest one attorney in particular. They should present a list of excellent attorneys to the donor, if asked. The nonprofit never pays the donor's legal fees.

11. B: Soft credit means the gift came from both spouses, even though only one check was issued.

12. B: A development director should never speculate about the status of a prospect's life. Even though donor files are confidential, you never know who might read them.

13. A: It is estimated that about 30% of the people in a database move during a calendar year. Their phone numbers also change at the same rate, so an annual update is recommended.

14. A: A nonprofit should run its database through National Change of Address (NCOA) or have its direct mail vendor do it.

15. B: Don't speculate. Use the gender code the donor directs you to use.

16. B: A 990 reveals a nonprofit's financial stability and its expenses. Donors can make decisions about donations by evaluating a nonprofit's salaries and expenditures.

17. C: Part of a charitable gift annuity payment comes from the donor's principal. Because it doesn't involve a capital gain, it's not taxable.

18. A: A nonprofit should never reveal what a donor has given to honor a friend, especially to the friend.

19. A: All charitable gift annuity rates are set by the American Council on Gift Annuities.

20. B: Using a national organization to set rates helps nonprofits compete for annuity customers.

21. C: If the nonprofit arranges for the appraisal, it could be answerable to the Internal Revenue Service (IRS) if it's discovered that the appraisal was performed dishonestly. A donor should schedule and pay for the painting's appraisal, and the donor will be responsible for any disagreements with the IRS about its value.

22. A: Advisory board members can help a nonprofit get to know them before elevating them to the board of trustees.

23. D: When a donor sends a premium payment to the nonprofit and the nonprofit makes the payment, the donor's premium is treated like a gift.

24. B: An insurance policy's beneficiaries are easily changeable. A nonprofit might be taken out of the list of beneficiaries and not be aware of it.

25. A: Consistency is everything when rating a donor.

26. C: Individuals make up the lion's share of total giving.

27. A: A charitable lead trust pays its income to a charity for a period of years, and when that term is over, the payments revert to whomever the trustee chooses.

28. B: Charities are exempt from the No Call List regulations, but the donor is saying he or she doesn't want to be called, so the file should reflect these wishes.

29. C: Many employers will not match gifts to churches or national church headquarters.

30. A: Participation rates can indicate how much a university's alumni value their alma mater.

31. D: Baby boomer women give approximately 89% more to charity than men, according to a 2012 study by the Women's Philanthropy Institute.

32. A: Some donors ask for a nonprofit's annual gift to gauge how generously its other donors behave.

33. B: Transferring ownership of the stock to a nonprofit avoids all capital gains taxes.

34. A: Payroll and federated campaigns have been active for decades.

35. D: Philanthropy indicates more dollars raised over a longer period of time to make a significant impact.

36. A: A board should not manage the day-to-day operation of a nonprofit. Instead, a board governs with policies and bylaws that are established to follow the nonprofit's mission.

37. C: Purchasing mailing lists returns very few qualified potential donors.

38. A: A gift acceptance policy guides development officers to make the right decisions about what gifts to accept and how to process them.

39. B: When a nonprofit organizes an auction or a gambling night, the Internal Revenue Service does not permit successful auction bids or games of chance winnings to be tax deductible because (1) in an auction the bidder is paying for donated goods or services, and (2) participants who gamble anticipate winning money. Tax-deductible contributions must be non-quid pro quo.

40. C: Their bequest gifts can be many times larger than their annual or capital gifts.

41. B: Someone may be inclined to give but does not have the resources. Another person may have vast financial resources but has no inclination to give. A good prospect must be financially capable and highly inclined to give.

42. D: Studying the dates and types of moves can reveal what more can be done to cultivate a donor or prospect better.

43. A: If assets are held in a private trust, it's impossible to discover what they are and how they are valued.

44. C: There is no difference in giving among races.

45. A: Donor assignment is a group discussion; it should be revisited periodically, and reassignments may occur.

46. C: Because most annual fund pledges are verbal, if they go unpaid by year end, they are "washed" or cancelled by the database. They will be invited to make a new pledge in the following year.

47. B: Nonprofits and universities base their construction loans on the pledges or contracts they receive from donors. They are considered legally enforceable. The courts look more favorably on nonprofits as plaintiffs now than they have in years past in unpaid pledge cases.

48. B: If the original purpose of the bequest cannot now be fulfilled because programs, technology, and structures change, it benefits the nonprofit to work with the family to try to fulfill the donor's intent in other ways. If no communication occurs, families have been known to sue to claw back entire bequests.

49. C: Never share other peoples' personal information with donors.

50. B: The nonprofit staff can take these encounters back to the public relations or marketing department that can decide how it may create public images to reflect its contemporary mission and services based on clients' needs. Correcting false assumptions can change donors' minds but only after the messages have time to sink in.

How to Overcome Test Anxiety

Just the thought of taking a test is enough to make most people a little nervous. A test is an important event that can have a long-term impact on your future, so it's important to take it seriously and it's natural to feel anxious about performing well. But just because anxiety is normal, that doesn't mean that it's helpful in test taking, or that you should simply accept it as part of your life. Anxiety can have a variety of effects. These effects can be mild, like making you feel slightly nervous, or severe, like blocking your ability to focus or remember even a simple detail.

If you experience test anxiety—whether severe or mild—it's important to know how to beat it. To discover this, first you need to understand what causes test anxiety.

Causes of Test Anxiety

While we often think of anxiety as an uncontrollable emotional state, it can actually be caused by simple, practical things. One of the most common causes of test anxiety is that a person does not feel adequately prepared for their test. This feeling can be the result of many different issues such as poor study habits or lack of organization, but the most common culprit is time management. Starting to study too late, failing to organize your study time to cover all of the material, or being distracted while you study will mean that you're not well prepared for the test. This may lead to cramming the night before, which will cause you to be physically and mentally exhausted for the test. Poor time management also contributes to feelings of stress, fear, and hopelessness as you realize you are not well prepared but don't know what to do about it.

Other times, test anxiety is not related to your preparation for the test but comes from unresolved fear. This may be a past failure on a test, or poor performance on tests in general. It may come from comparing yourself to others who seem to be performing better or from the stress of living up to expectations. Anxiety may be driven by fears of the future—how failure on this test would affect your educational and career goals. These fears are often completely irrational, but they can still negatively impact your test performance.

> **Review Video:** <u>3 Reasons You Have Test Anxiety</u>
> Visit mometrix.com/academy and enter code: 428468

Elements of Test Anxiety

As mentioned earlier, test anxiety is considered to be an emotional state, but it has physical and mental components as well. Sometimes you may not even realize that you are suffering from test anxiety until you notice the physical symptoms. These can include trembling hands, rapid heartbeat, sweating, nausea, and tense muscles. Extreme anxiety may lead to fainting or vomiting. Obviously, any of these symptoms can have a negative impact on testing. It is important to recognize them as soon as they begin to occur so that you can address the problem before it damages your performance.

> **Review Video:** <u>3 Ways to Tell You Have Test Anxiety</u>
> Visit mometrix.com/academy and enter code: 927847

The mental components of test anxiety include trouble focusing and inability to remember learned information. During a test, your mind is on high alert, which can help you recall information and stay focused for an extended period of time. However, anxiety interferes with your mind's natural processes, causing you to blank out, even on the questions you know well. The strain of testing during anxiety makes it difficult to stay focused, especially on a test that may take several hours. Extreme anxiety can take a huge mental toll, making it difficult not only to recall test information but even to understand the test questions or pull your thoughts together.

> **Review Video:** <u>How Test Anxiety Affects Memory</u>
> Visit mometrix.com/academy and enter code: 609003

Effects of Test Anxiety

Test anxiety is like a disease—if left untreated, it will get progressively worse. Anxiety leads to poor performance, and this reinforces the feelings of fear and failure, which in turn lead to poor performances on subsequent tests. It can grow from a mild nervousness to a crippling condition. If allowed to progress, test anxiety can have a big impact on your schooling, and consequently on your future.

Test anxiety can spread to other parts of your life. Anxiety on tests can become anxiety in any stressful situation, and blanking on a test can turn into panicking in a job situation. But fortunately, you don't have to let anxiety rule your testing and determine your grades. There are a number of relatively simple steps you can take to move past anxiety and function normally on a test and in the rest of life.

> **Review Video:** <u>How Test Anxiety Impacts Your Grades</u>
> Visit mometrix.com/academy and enter code: 939819

Physical Steps for Beating Test Anxiety

While test anxiety is a serious problem, the good news is that it can be overcome. It doesn't have to control your ability to think and remember information. While it may take time, you can begin taking steps today to beat anxiety.

Just as your first hint that you may be struggling with anxiety comes from the physical symptoms, the first step to treating it is also physical. Rest is crucial for having a clear, strong mind. If you are tired, it is much easier to give in to anxiety. But if you establish good sleep habits, your body and mind will be ready to perform optimally, without the strain of exhaustion. Additionally, sleeping well helps you to retain information better, so you're more likely to recall the answers when you see the test questions.

Getting good sleep means more than going to bed on time. It's important to allow your brain time to relax. Take study breaks from time to time so it doesn't get overworked, and don't study right before bed. Take time to rest your mind before trying to rest your body, or you may find it difficult to fall asleep.

> **Review Video:** <u>The Importance of Sleep for Your Brain</u>
> Visit mometrix.com/academy and enter code: 319338

Along with sleep, other aspects of physical health are important in preparing for a test. Good nutrition is vital for good brain function. Sugary foods and drinks may give a burst of energy but this burst is followed by a crash, both physically and emotionally. Instead, fuel your body with protein and vitamin-rich foods.

Also, drink plenty of water. Dehydration can lead to headaches and exhaustion, especially if your brain is already under stress from the rigors of the test. Particularly if your test is a long one, drink water during the breaks. And if possible, take an energy-boosting snack to eat between sections.

> **Review Video:** <u>How Diet Can Affect your Mood</u>
> Visit mometrix.com/academy and enter code: 624317

Along with sleep and diet, a third important part of physical health is exercise. Maintaining a steady workout schedule is helpful, but even taking 5-minute study breaks to walk can help get your blood pumping faster and clear your head. Exercise also releases endorphins, which contribute to a positive feeling and can help combat test anxiety.

When you nurture your physical health, you are also contributing to your mental health. If your body is healthy, your mind is much more likely to be healthy as well. So take time to rest, nourish your body with healthy food and water, and get moving as much as possible. Taking these physical steps will make you stronger and more able to take the mental steps necessary to overcome test anxiety.

> **Review Video:** <u>How to Stay Healthy and Prevent Test Anxiety</u>
> Visit mometrix.com/academy and enter code: 877894

Mental Steps for Beating Test Anxiety

Working on the mental side of test anxiety can be more challenging, but as with the physical side, there are clear steps you can take to overcome it. As mentioned earlier, test anxiety often stems from lack of preparation, so the obvious solution is to prepare for the test. Effective studying may be the most important weapon you have for beating test anxiety, but you can and should employ several other mental tools to combat fear.

First, boost your confidence by reminding yourself of past success—tests or projects that you aced. If you're putting as much effort into preparing for this test as you did for those, there's no reason you should expect to fail here. Work hard to prepare; then trust your preparation.

Second, surround yourself with encouraging people. It can be helpful to find a study group, but be sure that the people you're around will encourage a positive attitude. If you spend time with others who are anxious or cynical, this will only contribute to your own anxiety. Look for others who are motivated to study hard from a desire to succeed, not from a fear of failure.

Third, reward yourself. A test is physically and mentally tiring, even without anxiety, and it can be helpful to have something to look forward to. Plan an activity following the test, regardless of the outcome, such as going to a movie or getting ice cream.

When you are taking the test, if you find yourself beginning to feel anxious, remind yourself that you know the material. Visualize successfully completing the test. Then take a few deep, relaxing breaths and return to it. Work through the questions carefully but with confidence, knowing that you are capable of succeeding.

Developing a healthy mental approach to test taking will also aid in other areas of life. Test anxiety affects more than just the actual test—it can be damaging to your mental health and even contribute to depression. It's important to beat test anxiety before it becomes a problem for more than testing.

> **Review Video:** <u>**Test Anxiety and Depression**</u>
> Visit mometrix.com/academy and enter code: 904704

Study Strategy

Being prepared for the test is necessary to combat anxiety, but what does being prepared look like? You may study for hours on end and still not feel prepared. What you need is a strategy for test prep. The next few pages outline our recommended steps to help you plan out and conquer the challenge of preparation.

Step 1: Scope Out the Test

Learn everything you can about the format (multiple choice, essay, etc.) and what will be on the test. Gather any study materials, course outlines, or sample exams that may be available. Not only will this help you to prepare, but knowing what to expect can help to alleviate test anxiety.

Step 2: Map Out the Material

Look through the textbook or study guide and make note of how many chapters or sections it has. Then divide these over the time you have. For example, if a book has 15 chapters and you have five days to study, you need to cover three chapters each day. Even better, if you have the time, leave an extra day at the end for overall review after you have gone through the material in depth.

If time is limited, you may need to prioritize the material. Look through it and make note of which sections you think you already have a good grasp on, and which need review. While you are studying, skim quickly through the familiar sections and take more time on the challenging parts. Write out your plan so you don't get lost as you go. Having a written plan also helps you feel more in control of the study, so anxiety is less likely to arise from feeling overwhelmed at the amount to cover.

Step 3: Gather Your Tools

Decide what study method works best for you. Do you prefer to highlight in the book as you study and then go back over the highlighted portions? Or do you type out notes of the important information? Or is it helpful to make flashcards that you can carry with you? Assemble the pens, index cards, highlighters, post-it notes, and any other materials you may need so you won't be distracted by getting up to find things while you study.

If you're having a hard time retaining the information or organizing your notes, experiment with different methods. For example, try color-coding by subject with colored pens, highlighters, or post-it notes. If you learn better by hearing, try recording yourself reading your notes so you can listen while in the car, working out, or simply sitting at your desk. Ask a friend to quiz you from your flashcards, or try teaching someone the material to solidify it in your mind.

Step 4: Create Your Environment

It's important to avoid distractions while you study. This includes both the obvious distractions like visitors and the subtle distractions like an uncomfortable chair (or a too-comfortable couch that makes you want to fall asleep). Set up the best study environment possible: good lighting and a comfortable work area. If background music helps you focus, you may want to turn it on, but otherwise keep the room quiet. If you are using a computer to take notes, be sure you don't have any other windows open, especially applications like social media, games, or anything else that could distract you. Silence your phone and turn off notifications. Be sure to keep water close by so you stay hydrated while you study (but avoid unhealthy drinks and snacks).

Also, take into account the best time of day to study. Are you freshest first thing in the morning? Try to set aside some time then to work through the material. Is your mind clearer in the afternoon or evening? Schedule your study session then. Another method is to study at the same time of day that you will take the test, so that your brain gets used to working on the material at that time and will be ready to focus at test time.

Step 5: Study!

Once you have done all the study preparation, it's time to settle into the actual studying. Sit down, take a few moments to settle your mind so you can focus, and begin to follow your study plan. Don't give in to distractions or let yourself procrastinate. This is your time to prepare so you'll be ready to fearlessly approach the test. Make the most of the time and stay focused.

Of course, you don't want to burn out. If you study too long you may find that you're not retaining the information very well. Take regular study breaks. For example, taking five minutes out of every hour to walk briskly, breathing deeply and swinging your arms, can help your mind stay fresh.

As you get to the end of each chapter or section, it's a good idea to do a quick review. Remind yourself of what you learned and work on any difficult parts. When you feel that you've mastered the material, move on to the next part. At the end of your study session, briefly skim through your notes again.

But while review is helpful, cramming last minute is NOT. If at all possible, work ahead so that you won't need to fit all your study into the last day. Cramming overloads your brain with more information than it can process and retain, and your tired mind may struggle to recall even previously learned information when it is overwhelmed with last-minute study. Also, the urgent nature of cramming and the stress placed on your brain contribute to anxiety. You'll be more likely to go to the test feeling unprepared and having trouble thinking clearly.

So don't cram, and don't stay up late before the test, even just to review your notes at a leisurely pace. Your brain needs rest more than it needs to go over the information again. In fact, plan to finish your studies by noon or early afternoon the day before the test. Give your brain the rest of the day to relax or focus on other things, and get a good night's sleep. Then you will be fresh for the test and better able to recall what you've studied.

Step 6: Take a practice test

Many courses offer sample tests, either online or in the study materials. This is an excellent resource to check whether you have mastered the material, as well as to prepare for the test format and environment.

Check the test format ahead of time: the number of questions, the type (multiple choice, free response, etc.), and the time limit. Then create a plan for working through them. For example, if you have 30 minutes to take a 60-question test, your limit is 30 seconds per question. Spend less time on the questions you know well so that you can take more time on the difficult ones.

If you have time to take several practice tests, take the first one open book, with no time limit. Work through the questions at your own pace and make sure you fully understand them. Gradually work up to taking a test under test conditions: sit at a desk with all study materials put away and set a timer. Pace yourself to make sure you finish the test with time to spare and go back to check your answers if you have time.

After each test, check your answers. On the questions you missed, be sure you understand why you missed them. Did you misread the question (tests can use tricky wording)? Did you forget the information? Or was it something you hadn't learned? Go back and study any shaky areas that the practice tests reveal.

Taking these tests not only helps with your grade, but also aids in combating test anxiety. If you're already used to the test conditions, you're less likely to worry about it, and working through tests until you're scoring well gives you a confidence boost. Go through the practice tests until you feel comfortable, and then you can go into the test knowing that you're ready for it.

Test Tips

On test day, you should be confident, knowing that you've prepared well and are ready to answer the questions. But aside from preparation, there are several test day strategies you can employ to maximize your performance.

First, as stated before, get a good night's sleep the night before the test (and for several nights before that, if possible). Go into the test with a fresh, alert mind rather than staying up late to study.

Try not to change too much about your normal routine on the day of the test. It's important to eat a nutritious breakfast, but if you normally don't eat breakfast at all, consider eating just a protein bar. If you're a coffee drinker, go ahead and have your normal coffee. Just make sure you time it so that the caffeine doesn't wear off right in the middle of your test. Avoid sugary beverages, and drink enough water to stay hydrated but not so much that you need a restroom break 10 minutes into the test. If your test isn't first thing in the morning, consider going for a walk or doing a light workout before the test to get your blood flowing.

Allow yourself enough time to get ready, and leave for the test with plenty of time to spare so you won't have the anxiety of scrambling to arrive in time. Another reason to be early is to select a good seat. It's helpful to sit away from doors and windows, which can be distracting. Find a good seat, get out your supplies, and settle your mind before the test begins.

When the test begins, start by going over the instructions carefully, even if you already know what to expect. Make sure you avoid any careless mistakes by following the directions.

Then begin working through the questions, pacing yourself as you've practiced. If you're not sure on an answer, don't spend too much time on it, and don't let it shake your confidence. Either skip it and come back later, or eliminate as many wrong answers as possible and guess among the remaining ones. Don't dwell on these questions as you continue—put them out of your mind and focus on what lies ahead.

Be sure to read all of the answer choices, even if you're sure the first one is the right answer. Sometimes you'll find a better one if you keep reading. But don't second-guess yourself if you do immediately know the answer. Your gut instinct is usually right. Don't let test anxiety rob you of the information you know.

If you have time at the end of the test (and if the test format allows), go back and review your answers. Be cautious about changing any, since your first instinct tends to be correct, but make sure you didn't misread any of the questions or accidentally mark the wrong answer choice. Look over any you skipped and make an educated guess.

At the end, leave the test feeling confident. You've done your best, so don't waste time worrying about your performance or wishing you could change anything. Instead, celebrate the successful completion of this test. And finally, use this test to learn how to deal with anxiety even better next time.

Important Qualification

Not all anxiety is created equal. If your test anxiety is causing major issues in your life beyond the classroom or testing center, or if you are experiencing troubling physical symptoms related to your anxiety, it may be a sign of a serious physiological or psychological condition. If this sounds like your situation, we strongly encourage you to seek professional help.

Thank You

We at Mometrix would like to extend our heartfelt thanks to you, our friend and patron, for allowing us to play a part in your journey. It is a privilege to serve people from all walks of life who are unified in their commitment to building the best future they can for themselves.

The preparation you devote to these important testing milestones may be the most valuable educational opportunity you have for making a real difference in your life. We encourage you to put your heart into it—that feeling of succeeding, overcoming, and yes, conquering will be well worth the hours you've invested.

We want to hear your story, your struggles and your successes, and if you see any opportunities for us to improve our materials so we can help others even more effectively in the future, please share that with us as well. **The team at Mometrix would be absolutely thrilled to hear from you!** So please, send us an email (support@mometrix.com) and let's stay in touch.

If you'd like some additional help, check out these other resources we offer for your exam:

http://MometrixFlashcards.com/CFRE

124

Additional Bonus Material

Due to our efforts to try to keep this book to a manageable length, we've created a link that will give you access to all of your additional bonus material.

Please visit https://www.mometrix.com/bonus948/cfre to access the information.